Taking the Norfolk Air

BBC Radio Norfolk,
the first 25 years

BBC RADIO NORFOLK

Published by
Grice Chapman Publishing
The Shire House, Burgh next Aylsham
Norwich, NR11 6TP
www.gricechapman.com
Grice Chapman is a division of the Evergreen Media Group

ISBN 0-9545726-7-X

Designed and printed in England by
Barnwell's Print Ltd, Printing Works
2-6 Penfold Street, Aylsham, Norfolk, NR11 6ET
Telephone: +44 (0)1263 732767

Foreword
Martin Brundle

Back in 1980, when BBC Radio Norfolk began transmitting to our beloved county, I thought it all seemed very exotic. At the time I was very much an amateur competition driver, expecting to be selling cars for the rest of my life, rather than racing them and then becoming a Formula One commentator. Being approached by the King's Lynn branch for an interview about my career was very exciting. I remember going up to the studio on the first floor in the corner of the Tuesday Market Place to what seemed to be a 'one-man band' and very much an outpost. The double-glazing was almost effective in keeping out the road traffic noise, until a truck went past and everything vibrated.

Nevertheless, it was great to hear local and regional news, information and sport from this very special county of ours. We are rather insular over here and quite clearly the fact that you cannot pass through Norfolk – you either visit it or you don't – leaves us with a particular pace of life and image to the rest of the world. We can appear somewhat cool and unfriendly, but we are not, and Radio Norfolk has proved a great way of showing that.

As we have a very rural environment with few chimney pots and plenty of open countryside, the social benefit of focussed local media is doubly important. The fact that many of the presenters have become household names in the region demonstrates the popularity and importance of the content, information, style and entertainment Radio Norfolk provides.

Without doubt, that local media helped me establish my motor-racing career. Radio Norfolk, and particularly David Clayton, supported me along the way. Whatever I achieved, they were there to record it and to help me on to the next rung of the ladder, whether it was at an outside broadcast in the King's Lynn town centre or at the British Grand Prix. David even followed me to the German Grand Prix on one occasion. Of course, I am just one of numerous sportsmen and – women who have benefited from local radio coverage.

Being based in Norfolk, but having worldwide ambitions, you need a good springboard to generate success, and I certainly enjoyed that help. I only wish I had more time to be involved in other programmes, particularly as I have a good face for radio. I did, though, host a sports quiz show and record a lengthy *Desert Island Discs*-style of programme on the eve of my best Grand Prix season in 1992.

I am often asked what I miss most about my home area when I am travelling the world, and I always respond 'the Norfolk accent'. The local characters, particularly the older ones with a strong Norfolk dialect, are just full of fascinating stories of life's experiences. True Norfolk people have a genuine integrity and warmth, and this is very well reflected by Radio Norfolk. They richly deserve the accolade of being one of the top performing local radio stations in the country and I am sure they will continue to do so for significantly more than the next 25 years.

Martin Brundle
September 2005

Contents

Introduction
David Clayton

To those of us who have been involved from the start, it hardly seems possible that Norfolk's 'new neighbour', as we were labelled back in the autumn of 1980, can possibly have reached the maturity of a 25th birthday. BBC Radio Norfolk first went on air on 11 September in that year. Sadly, that date in the calendar has taken on a different significance in recent times.

The intention of this birthday publication is to capture some of the moments in 25 years of broadcasting to the people of Norfolk. The book is not meant to be a perfect chronological record of the radio station, nor is it a complete anthology of everything we've done. It is more a collection of stories that, put together, encapsulate life on Norfolk's first local radio station. I hope it also provides some insight into what we do and how we do it.

It would be impossible to find room for everyone who has been involved with BBC Radio Norfolk to be able to write a chapter, or even a paragraph, but whilst we've entrusted various sections of the book to certain individuals, we have drawn in other stories and anecdotes from many staff, past and present, so I thank them for their time and their memories. Thanks are also due to the many contributors, interviewees and regular guests who have graced our studios over the years, but particularly to our listeners.

Since the station went on air, we have been blessed with a large and enthusiastic audience. Radio Norfolk has always been one of the BBC's most successful local radio stations, at times enjoying the number one spot. While it would be quite right to pay tribute to the past and present broadcasters for that, it is perhaps more important to acknowledge the way in which the people of Norfolk have listened to, joined in with and, in many ways, cherished their BBC local radio station.

Of course, the broadcasting landscape has changed a great deal since we first went on air. In 1980, we were on our own. Not only are there now more local commercial stations in

Norfolk, but the BBC's networks have grown in popularity too. Then there is the internet, high quality digital audio broadcasting (DAB), and worldwide radio stations available via satellite. With all this competition growing apace, the young broadcasters who form part of the talented team at today's Radio Norfolk face the challenge of the next 25 years.

I would like to record special thanks to John Mills, Wally Webb, Chris Goreham, Sarah Kings, Jill Bennett, Matthew Gudgin, Graham Barnard, Tony Mallion, Peter Cook and Tim Bishop, all of whom were happily press-ganged into taking charge of sections of this book. Many thanks also to Bridget Bagshaw, who undertook the painstaking task of editing the manuscript.

You'll be happy to know that by buying this book you've helped the BBC Radio Norfolk Helpline Charity Trust. Over some 19 years, the Trust has raised over £80,000 for local causes.

When you read on, you'll discover how I came to make the tea one Sunday morning back in September 1980, and so you will understand how absolutely proud I am to be able to write this introduction to a 25th-birthday publication as BBC Radio Norfolk's editor. Enjoy the book and thank you for buying it.

David Clayton
September 2005

Chapter 1
How it all began
David Clayton

I should not have been there, but I sneaked in on the pretext of handing over to Rob Bonnet a tape I had made interviewing the finalist of the Miss British Isles competition at Great Yarmouth. On the previous evening I'd had the good fortune to be the compère of the show at Yarmouth's Wellington Pier – the person in the dinner jacket and bow tie who gets to interview the swim-suited contestants.

So getting hold of the excited and rather lovely finalist and persuading her to talk into a tape machine borrowed from Hospital Radio Norwich – where I was doing regular programmes for hospital patients in Norfolk – was easy. I had an 'exclusive', and Rob had succumbed to my persuasion that BBC Radio Norfolk would want it on their airwaves on their first day. Rob is now one of the regular faces of sport on television on BBC1, but then was a newly recruited producer on the embryonic BBC Radio Norfolk, the first of a new wave of county radio stations.

It was Thursday 11 September 1980 – the day Radio Norfolk officially began broadcasting to an expectant county. Rob was predictably a bit busy, as were his fellow producers, running around with a bagful of nerves and apprehension as the transmitters were switched on. To complicate matters, and adding to the tension, Radio Norfolk was arriving into the world live on television. BBC TV's *Look East* programme thought it such an important moment in regional broadcasting history that they had set up their cameras in the studios ready to capture the moment.

Someone hastily took my tape of the beauty queen – I forget who – promising it would get to Rob. It didn't, and was never heard, which was just as well as I'd recorded it at the wrong tape speed. This had happened on the advice of Keith Skipper, one of the new Radio Norfolk producers, poached from the *Eastern Daily Press*. I think I made the mistake of

Jockeying for the jockey: Rob Bonnet at Yarmouth Races

asking him the right speed at which the tape recorder should run. He told me. He was wrong. Rob later advised me against asking Skip technical questions, and Skip himself said later, 'Never ask *me* for technical advice!'

The BBC had introduced its local radio stations in waves and BBC Radio Norfolk was one of a new breed – a slimmed down version of those that had paved the way, starting with BBC Radio Leicester in November 1967.

The BBC had long made a name for itself with network radio, but it took a distinguished BBC man, Frank Gillard, director of sound broadcasting and a former war correspondent, to spot the potential of a local radio service. He had been to the United States and seen the impact local stations had in smaller communities. Could it happen in Britain? Frank was convinced it could. He set about some serious lobbying and, as we emerged from the austere days of the fifties, a special report was commissioned to look at the future of broadcasting. This was the Pilkington Report, which recognised the BBC had a case for local radio. That was fine on paper, but what would it – and what could it – sound like?

In 1962, the BBC set about mocking-up some local radio dummy runs in 16 different towns and cities to persuade the Pilkington Committee that the idea was worth backing. In the way these things tend to work, the government did nothing for a while, but then gave the go-ahead in late 1966 for the BBC to get started. So it did, the following year. Commercial radio came along a little later.

In research for such programmes on Radio Norfolk as *The Norfolk Years*, I've come across old newspaper reports about council meetings. Normally they're a bit tedious to plod through, but I spotted some about local radio. It appears the

BBC approached various cities and large conurbations, offering them the chance of a kind of partnership on local radio. With a little bit of funding from a local authority and some from the BBC coffers, there might just be enough money to set up a small local station. They debated this concept in Norwich's council chamber, and whilst some councillors thought it a good thing, others predictably did not. In the end it did not matter, because Norwich was not chosen for the first group of stations launched back in 1967. Leicester took the accolade, and the Postmaster General declared a new era of broadcasting well and truly open on 8 November that year.

Fast-forwarding to the mid-seventies, I was on holiday in my native Yorkshire and tuning into BBC Radio Teeside, based in Middlesbrough, a station that made it to air in 1971. These days it is known as BBC Radio Cleveland. I was absolutely mesmerised by what I heard. Compared with my usual listening on Radio 1, it was so informal, distinctive and full of people with accents like mine used to be. I couldn't turn it off.

While my wife went shopping, I blagged my way in to have a look round its first floor studios on Linthorpe Road in Middlesbrough. The nice chap who thought I was important enough to show round let me sit in one of the studios as someone came in to read a news bulletin. To this day, I cannot explain the tingle of excitement I felt to be in the presence of live radio as it happened.

So you're thinking, what an anorak! Well, it's true. I went straight home from my holiday and penned a letter to the only local media we had. The *Eastern Daily Press* took the full force of my written disappointment that we did not have such a station in Norfolk. The newspaper printed my letter, and I felt a little better that my voice had been heard.

At the time we did have in Norwich a sort of local radio service coming out of the BBC premises in All Saints Green. The programme, *Roundabout East Anglia*, was on the air every weekday morning between 6.45 and 8.45 as a regional Radio 4 alternative to the *Today* programme. It covered the same area as *Look East*, so wasn't truly local. Broadcasters like Ellis Hill, Christopher Trace, Tom Edwards and John Mountford presented the programmes, which were more of a serious news magazine format, and lacked the informality and accessibility of real local radio. After all, the programme was a clone of Radio 4. But my mother loved it, and took a real shine to the very professional Ellis Hill. The man who steered the *Roundabout East Anglia* ship for many years, until its demise, was Michael Chapman. He, along with John Mills, John Mountford and Phil Johnson, were eventually to cross the road to the new local radio station when it opened.

So onward to 1979, when word got out that a BBC local radio station for Norfolk was planned to start in the autumn of 1980. Joy! Whilst budding DJs like me were getting all excited and expectant, the truth behind how Norfolk landed a BBC station in 1980 only became known much later.

Michael Barton was, at the time, the BBC's controller of local radio and it was he who negotiated with the government and the chaps from commercial local radio as to how the broadcasting areas of the country were to be carved up. Quite rightly, the commercial sector and the BBC did not want to launch side by side in the same location at the same time. Much better to open a BBC station in one place and a commercial station in another, so as to build a good audience base before the opposition came along.

I have had the pleasure of knowing Michael for many years. He is now a much respected elder statesman of broadcasting, and I had no reason to disbelieve him when he revealed that BBC Radio Norfolk's existence, ahead of a commercial station, was settled in an unconventional way, to say the least. In most cases, the commercial chaps and the BBC agreed locations each time the creation of more stations were being considered, but when Devon and Norfolk were suggested, both parties declared a strong interest in opening a new radio station first – so who should it be? Unable to reach an agreement, the Home Secretary of the time, Willie Whitelaw, tossed a coin. Michael Barton called 'tails', won and staked his claim on Norfolk, while John Thompson, for the Independent Broadcasting Authority, accepted Devon.

The BBC had not opened a local radio station for many years – this really was a new era and money was tight. Plans were drawn up, but the proposed cost shook the director general, so they had to be redrawn, creating an inevitable delay. The first BBC local radio stations had started with a staff of around 30, but those in the new wave, including Norfolk, had to be leaner and meaner. There was another spin-off from tightening the purse strings; the radio studios were designed with what we call 'self-opping' in mind. That is, the presenters worked the controls of the radio consoles themselves. Earlier stations had extra station assistants to drive most of the programmes. Not at Norfolk.

Norfolk Tower: not a pretty sight but our first home

So why did the aptly named Norfolk Tower on Surrey Street become the station's original home? In all sorts of ways it wasn't ideal. It was a good way from the main shopping streets of Norwich, and, to many, was an unattractive office building. 'Functional' might be a kinder description. For reasons I never quite understood, an illuminated BBC Radio Norfolk sign sat around the radio station's garage for years. We were not allowed to attach it to the outside of the building to let people know where we were. So Radio Norfolk was a little anonymous, sharing, as it did, an entrance with the rest of the Tower's tenants.

Across Surrey Street were the BBC premises in All Saints Green, from where *Look East* was transmitted and the *Roundabout East Anglia* programmes broadcast. Could not have BBC Radio Norfolk been housed in the BBC's elegant converted Georgian mansion, known as St Catherine's Close? Could it be squeezed into an already full building? I think I saw a set of optimistic plans gathering dust in later years, but at the time the answer was 'no'.

But the ground floor of Norfolk Tower was available. While the L-shape of the accommodation was not ideal, the BBC had found a place with more room than 20 or so people might need, so a studio block was constructed within the space, with sound-proofing walls to cocoon the broadcasters in the necessary silence. Being close to the *Look East* building, the new Radio Norfolk could easily be hooked up to the BBC's existing technical systems.

Inside Norfolk Tower: before we brought it to life

So at the beginning of 1980, the station's first manager was appointed. He was, by his own admission, a casualty from a news and current affairs reshuffle at Broadcasting House in London. Mike Chaney was a stalwart of the *Today* programme, but his services were no longer needed. In the bargaining that accompanied his departure, he was promised the managership of a local radio station. It was, in some ways, a controversial appointment in the corridors of local radio, but Mike was given the helm of the embryonic Radio Norfolk and immediately grabbed a chap he'd worked with in the *Today* office to be his news editor.

Ian Hyams actually lived in South Norfolk, and commuted from there to London, but was eager to spend more time in and around his home. The other member needed for the management team was a programme organiser. Mike again tried to raid the *Today* office, where he wanted to lift a talented producer, Roger Gale, for the Norwich job. But before Mike could sign him up, Roger was offered a plum job in children's television. As it happens Roger's career was to take a different turn much later, when he entered politics. He has been the Conservative MP for Thanet North in Kent since 1983.

So the next choice was Peter Glanville, who had impressed at his job interview, and was to bring to Norwich all his experience as an education producer from BBC Radio Medway (now Kent). The chief engineer, Dave Penney, also came from Kent.

The new bosses of Radio Norfolk decided some local consultation was called for. They had advertised and arranged a 'what-talents-have-you-got-that-we-might-want' evening at the Maid's Head Hotel in Norwich. I decided this was a 'must attend' event, and pitched up with a DJ mate, Stuart Graham, driving there in the big green Ford Transit van he used for transporting his disco.

It was a snowy night in April, but there were queues round the block. Somewhere else in the queue was Roy Waller. I didn't know him at the time, but he was trying to convince the BBC bosses they needed a local football commentator.

When we finally got to the front of the queue of hopefuls, we shuffled into a room where the four managers talked briefly to each person. In looks and stature, station manager Mike Chaney provided a more than passable impression of James Robertson Justice, the big bearded actor. Nearby was Peter Glanville, also bearded, while Ian Hyams was beardless. To say they were overwhelmed was something of an understatement. I declared my credentials as a local DJ, and so did Stuart. I think my name was scribbled on a piece of paper, along with my phone number, and that was that.

Then advertisements appeared in the *EDP* for the broadcasting jobs. They wanted producers – I applied. They wanted station assistants – I applied. Application forms arrived. I filled them in, totally convinced the Ocean Room in

Gorleston and Talk of East Anglia in Norwich were just the training grounds for budding BBC radio presenters. I was wrong. Duplicated letters landed on my mat at home thanking me for my interest, but no thanks – not even an interview! Rather in the ambitious way President Kennedy had declared America would make a moon landing by the end of the sixties, I had declared or perhaps even boasted to a girlfriend back in 1971 that I would be on radio in ten years. My declaration was looking very shaky – but she was no longer my girlfriend. I tried not to be disappointed.

During the summer of 1980 I was distracted and busy at the Ocean Room in Gorleston – too busy, in fact, to worry about not having a job with BBC Radio Norfolk. However others were being taken on. Mike Souter, for example, came south from his job on Radio Clyde in Scotland.

Meanwhile, unbeknown to me, the BBC was fitting out Norfolk Tower and its new hirelings were getting around the county in a Ford Cortina radio car. Lesley Dolphin, who is a Norfolk lass and had landed one of the jobs I wanted, recalls it was for her a dream come true to be working for the BBC in her home county. She spent her summer taking the radio car out to fêtes and carnivals, and dishing out leaflets about the soon-to-be-on-air Radio Norfolk. Everywhere she went, she was welcomed with open arms – an early indication of the popularity Radio Norfolk was to enjoy. The new staff were all despatched to the BBC's training establishment opposite Broadcasting House in London, and shown how to operate the equipment and produce programmes. They also regularly returned to Norfolk to learn a little more about the county.

There was an exciting moment when I realised that even though Radio Norfolk was not officially on air as such, it was carrying out test transmissions. One came from the Royal Norfolk Show. I tuned in and suddenly realised that spending a busy summer season at the Ocean Room was not what I really wanted to do. The broadcasters I heard – Bob Ledwidge, Mike Souter, Rob Bonnet, Keith Skipper and Neil Walker – were all having fun, and I wanted some of that, on the radio. I was feeling frustrated and jealous that I wasn't part of it.

Wally Webb was also listening in. We knew each other as fellow, or perhaps even rival, DJs around Norfolk. After the

Norfolk Show test transmissions, Radio Norfolk carried out more practice runs by letting their new producers have a go at a midday programme. Again I tuned in. By then Wally had got further than me by being interviewed for a producer's job, but was then turned down. He contacted Phil Johnson, one of the new station assistants – another job I didn't get – and was given a look round the studios. Then, by being in the right place at the right time, Wally bumped into Peter Glanville, was invited into his office and was offered a Sunday afternoon rock show for younger listeners. I would have been uncontrollably jealous, except that I knew nothing of this at the time.

Keith Roberts: in at the start

I was a partner in an entertainment agency as well as being a DJ and, one day during August 1980, another agent called me to say he'd been approached by someone at the BBC's new station to pick his brains about the local entertainment scene. My agent friend suggested I made the call back, as I knew something about radio. This I did, and spoke to one of the newly appointed producers, Keith Roberts. He invited me for a drink and we chatted. Michael Chapman, who knew me from my Hospital Radio Norwich activities, invited me to take part in a lunchtime test transmission to talk about showbiz in Norfolk. Then it was suggested I might pop in each Friday to do a regular showbiz round-up. At last I had a foot in the radio door.

Part of the new station's programme schedule included a 90-minute programme on a Sunday called *Talkback*. This was to be phone-in radio – very new to Norfolk. Listeners could debate a topic for half the time then give verdicts on some new record releases in the second 45 minutes, copying the style of *Juke Box Jury*. The plan was to include the opinions of a couple of local DJs. The first weekend producer, Bob Ledwidge, discovered what I did and invited me to join the panel. I was on air and loved it. I then persuaded him he really needed someone to make the tea and see the guests in each Sunday. I remember him hesitating, but in the end he gave in. He remembers now being far too busy to offer any resistance.

The opening night must have been full of tension. Not only was John Mountford set to open up the new Radio Norfolk with a special radio programme, but simultaneously broadcast on television as well. John remembers hearing the programme output in one ear of his headphones, instructions from his producer in the other and somehow having another earpiece inserted somewhere useful, taking the television director's talkback, so he knew when they were on air visually.

Despite 11 September being their wedding anniversary, Bob Ledwidge and his wife Liz were serving drinks and nibbles to the 'great and good' of Norfolk. While that was going on, several staff, including Wally Webb and Phil Johnson, were delegated to take 100 helium-filled balloons up to the first floor roof of Norfolk Tower and release them, once some trumpeters had blown a ceremonial launch fanfare live on television. This was duly done.

It had been hoped that the balloons would head skyward in a symbolic representation of meaningful messages heading out over the radio airwaves. In the event, as we came to learn from later experience, Norfolk Tower creates a strange wind vortex around the back of the building. On the calmest and warmest of days, a gale would blow around the back of the building. So it was on 11 September, when the balloons immediately swirled downwards and occupied the car park at the back of Norfolk Tower in a circular ground-hugging dance, but thankfully out of view of *Look East*'s cameras.

Big breakfast: A listener brings in a Norfolk dumpling for Terry Wogan to sample, Ian Hyams looks on with envy

The next morning – a Friday – Terry Wogan presented his Radio 2 show from Radio Norfolk's new studios, broadcasting to the nation *and* Norfolk, attracting that all-important publicity. Maggie Secker, who has been with Radio Norfolk since it began, found herself working on reception on the first Saturday morning. She remembers being surprised at the constant stream of people just wandering in, stopping, looking round and wandering out. Norfolk was coming to meet its new neighbour.

Where are they now?
John Mountford

So how did a son of the Staffordshire Potteries come to be waking up the innocent souls of Norfolk each weekday morning? Well, I'd fallen in love with the county two years previously, leaving my career with the BBC World Service at Bush House in London to present a daily regional Radio 4 programme from All Saints Green in Norwich. When the folks next door in Surrey Street began hatching plans for a brand new radio station, I was all ears.

Back to the future: John Mountford takes us to air

I cannot tell you how proud – and how terrified – I was to be chosen as the very first voice on air at Radio Norfolk's launch, and to return again before dawn next morning to host the breakfast show, a daily delight for the next two-and-a-half years.

Most things that listeners take for granted today were 'firsts' for us. I recall making the first live broadcasts from Thetford and from King's Lynn, and from a wherry and a waterbed. Mine was also the first 'cookery spot' – achieved by dragging a microphone cable the whole way through the building into the staff canteen. Nothing seemed impossible – and even if it was, we tried it anyway.

In the course of 'introducing the county to itself', I came to meet some fascinating people from all walks of life, and even a sprinkling of international celebrities. Oh, and one poor chap, who was dragged into my studio by an enthusiastic colleague, who had mistaken him for my next guest.

'So when did you become the captain of the world's biggest supertanker,' I asked.

'I didn't,' he replied, nonplussed. 'I'm a plumber – I just came in to dedicate a record to my mum.'

As Radio Norfolk's popularity rocketed, so too did my parallel career as the presenter of a regional BBC TV programme called *Weekend*. The programme's success led to other offers, most notably from the brand new BBC Breakfast TV, and from Esther Rantzen. For both I had to travel the length and breadth of the country and abroad. Keeping a daily date with Norfolk became impossible – and so it was with a heavy heart that I finally handed over the reins of the breakfast show.

For three years I relished travelling and reporting nationally, but then yet another parallel career, as the founder of a company producing radio commercials, asserted itself. The business had grown into one of the largest independent radio production companies in the country, and expanded into video production. Once again it was time to choose – between constant travel and spending more time with my business in Norfolk. This time the choice was easy. Today, I have recording studios in London and Norwich, a record label and an award-winning corporate video unit, yet I still live in Norfolk, and my two sons work with me in the business. What more could I wish for?

Where are they now?
Mike Souter

I'd come down by train from Glasgow, where I had spent three years as the action reporter at Radio Clyde. I'd parachuted, hang-glided, steeple-jacked and undertaken all sorts of similar madcap actions. Outside broadcasts and radio car were my speciality. It appeared that was exactly what Radio Norfolk wanted.

The bosses – Mike Chaney, Peter Glanville and Ian Hyams – all had colds, as did I. I just knew I had the job when the tin of throat pastilles was passed across the table of the room that was subsequently to become the station's record library.

'Norfolk is the graveyard of ambition,' said Mike Chaney. 'Once you are here, you'll never move on.'

Well, to an extent, he was right. I have maintained a house in Norfolk ever since. But, in recent years, I have specialised in leisure and tourism, and now make a living as a travel writer and broadcaster, spending at least six months of each year away from the county.

Before the station started broadcasting, we spent the summer of 1980 on a six-week training course at the Langham in London, opposite BBC Broadcasting House. There we learned how to operate what was then state-of-the-art stereo equipment. People forget how novel stereo broadcasting was in 1980, and we were the first BBC local radio station to broadcast in this revolutionary way.

At one point during the training we had a few days in Norfolk, to get to know our new patch. I was sent to visit a pig farm. For days afterwards, back in the warm of the London studios, a rural odour wafted up from my shoes. Lesson learnt. To this day I keep a pair of wellies in the back of the car.

Mike Chaney had this idea that we were not journalists, producers or station assistants. We were all part of a team and would all pitch in. My first job was to help Peter Glanville produce the first ever show. So many memories remain of that night: the young children who we selected to cut the ribbon live on television, and who I subsequently tracked down to reappear for our tenth anniversary; doing interviews with Norfolk, Virginia, and Norfolk Island, part of Australia; and Terry Wogan coming to do his breakfast show from our studios and arriving not a happy bunny, because the Maids Head Hotel had put him in a broom cupboard of a room.

The first programme that people really associate with me was *Hopscotch*, broadcast on a Saturday morning and in which I literally 'hopped' all over the county. I remain good friends with Roger Clarke from Acle, who we brought in as the Radio Norfolk vet and with Charles Henderson, who we inherited from *Roundabout East Anglia* as part of the gardening team, and I am still in contact with him in his retirement in Ireland.

One of my other main responsibilities was *Platform*, our Sunday afternoon arts show. What amazes me is how many people still come up to me and tell me they were interviewed on that programme. I often taped the second hour of the show and, one Sunday afternoon I was heading up the A17 to Scotland on leave, only to hear Roy Waller coming on and telling everyone that I was not in fact there – a trick he was to repeat time and time again, when I used to leave the studio for the weekend on a Friday afternoon to beat the traffic at the end of my afternoon show.

So many shows, so many memories. There is not one show or broadcasting job on the station I haven't done. My favourite? One was certainly presenting the breakfast show as a freelance in the early 1990s. My gardener said to me then that I must have been making a fortune. A total of £30 per day plus VAT it was, and that in an era when *Today in Norfolk* was a three-hour programme.

I also thoroughly enjoyed presenting the afternoon show in the mid-1980s and, although I am a morning person, *Mike Souter Late*, being all speech, was an extraordinary challenge. The idea of staying on air as long as there was something to talk about was amazing and we had some brilliant contributors, like Bren Knights, Rosemary Wakelin, Pat Cleary and Janette Hall, all of whom became extremely competent and well respected broadcasters. Having the key to Mr Salmon's cocktail cabinet, to relax after the show, made for a very convivial team, helped of course by Betty's cups of tea

Commanding role: Mike Souter

while we were on air. Being on the pitch to present a programme prior to the Milk Cup Final at Wembley remains an undoubted highlight, as was the interview I did with HRH the Prince of Wales in 1982, which became the main news story in the UK on August Bank Holiday Monday of that year. I remember too some DJ fellow coming in to produce demo tapes on a Sunday afternoon in the vacant studio, hoping to make his mark on the station one day. The one that got away? I decided that Bob Flowerdew's radical gardening ideas would never have wide appeal. Since then he has of course become one of our best respected gardening broadcasters.

Peter Franzen, the editor of the *Eastern Daily Press*, suggested to me recently that, when I was broadcasting in the mid-1980s, it was possibly the happiest time I have had in Norfolk. It was certainly the most fulfilling, challenging and stimulating.

That first day, 11 September 1980, was the start of so much – for me and for so many others, but it was 25 years ago and I am twice as old as I was then. And the DJ fellow, name of David Clayton, seems to have stuck with it. I knew he would get there one day!

Where are they now?
Mike Chaney

After leaving Norfolk Tower, I became a freelance broadcaster and journalist. I did a little television for BBC East and a great deal more radio reporting and presenting for Radio 4. But I am not a natural freelance and, even with the cushion of the BBC's pension, I needed regular work to keep the roof over our heads. So I became the director of communications for Southampton University for four years. When the opportunity came up to do the same job for Dorset County Council, I finally sold my Diss small-holding and the family moved down south.

I had another five years as a municipal spokesman and then the retirement clock chimed – and I inherited yet another pension. But as I had children still at university, I did another spell in public relations, this time at a smart Mayfair consultancy, where we all wore bow ties and red braces. But, as it will just when one is having fun, the clock ticked again – and now I am a pottering gardener living in a thatched cottage in a tiny village near the dramatic beauty of Dorset's coast, where I indulge my grandchildren and my wife's three cats.

Mike Chaney and his expanded family

Chapter 2
Parish pump and proud of it
John Mills

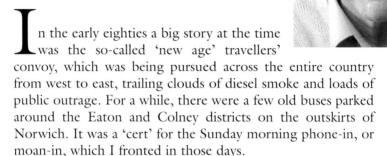

In the early eighties a big story at the time was the so-called 'new age' travellers' convoy, which was being pursued across the entire country from west to east, trailing clouds of diesel smoke and loads of public outrage. For a while, there were a few old buses parked around the Eaton and Colney districts on the outskirts of Norwich. It was a 'cert' for the Sunday morning phone-in, or moan-in, which I fronted in those days.

Now I'll let you into a little secret: although I had a reputation of being 'the man you love to hate', it was, to some degree, a bit of an act. So when a lady came on and started berating the travellers pitched on the open ground by her home for washing themselves in the stream that flowed through it, I gave her some real stick:

Me: Well they have to wash somewhere, don't they?
Her: Yes, but they take off all their clothes.
Me: Well you don't have to look, you know.
Her: But they're shameless. They dye their hair the most outrageous colours.
Me: Dyeing your hair is hardly a heinous crime – and not even that unusual.
Her: I'm not talking about the hair on their heads!

Ah, where would we be without the involvement of you, our audience? I have always believed that local radio is parish pump and proud of it – indeed it's our unofficial motto. Much more than any other part of the media, Radio Norfolk relates with – and, yes, relies on – our audience when compiling programmes. From the calls that come in, whether they are bringing events information, tip-offs to our news and travel teams, or simple goodwill messages, the listeners let us weave a web of sound that happily ensnares all who hear it. This relationship is unique; it's an airborne friendship, as David Clayton's tale underlines:

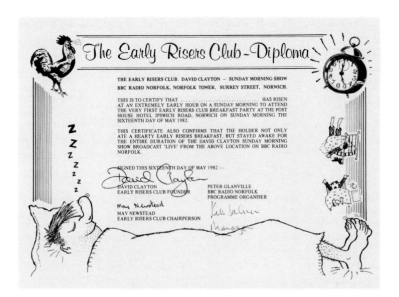

I was given the task of opening up Radio Norfolk on a Sunday morning in June 1981. There were a few religious tapes to play, a pile of records and what's on information. Those apart, I was on my own. Being something of a night owl, as a club DJ, I was pretty disoriented at 7 am, wondering who else, if anyone, might be up and about at this unearthly hour. But no one had said I couldn't use the phone lines, so I watched the switchboard light up like a Christmas tree.

First on the line was May Newstead from Cantley so, when the music stopped, I flicked a switch and we began chatting merrily on the air. Well, May was also the first caller the next week, and the next. On the Sunday after that, though, I decided a change was required, so I chose someone else to start the show. The phones went mad with people ringing in to see if May was all right!

That taught me something very important – that people are fascinated by other people more than anything else ... oh, and that there are loads of folk in Norfolk up and about at 7 am on a Sunday. And so the 'early risers club' was born, a group of like-minded listeners who tuned in to hear each other. Eventually, early risers' breakfasts were arranged at the Post

House hotel in Norwich, which led to members' organising their own get-togethers, mostly led by Billy and Marie Brighton.

If I learned anything from my early days on the radio, it was that broadcasting with people is much, much better than broadcasting to or at people.

Billy and Marie Brighton: no lie in

Up with the lark: members of the listener's 'early risers club'

Twenty years ago, when I presented Radio 4's *Feedback* programme, which is the network's equivalent of television's *Points of View*, I made the cardinal error, then, of referring to a listener-correspondent by his first name. He lost no time in giving me a piece of his mind for what he felt was an inexcusable liberty. It was surnames only, as far as he was concerned.

'But,' I protested, 'that's what we always do on local radio, so why not on network radio too?'

And lo, it did come to pass. Our lack of formality – less of the stuffed shirts of yesteryear – has spread across the airwaves. And long may it continue to break down the barriers of exclusivity.

Perhaps, though, you haven't always felt warmly towards the 'man you love to hate'? I vividly remember going out with my tape recorder to get the views of passers-by in Norwich's Gentleman's Walk. The subject doesn't matter, but the reaction does.

'Hello, I'm from Radio Norfolk. Do you mind if I ask you a couple of questions?'

He was my second or third victim.

'I know you. You're John Mills, aren't you?'

I preened. It's always heartening to be recognised by your voice alone. But then, without changing tone at all, he continued, 'I hate you, you know.'

Hearing Norfolk: John Mills

He still answered my question, though, which is the point I am making. Whether we are arguing the toss about a matter of the moment, or sharing the delights of a birthday greeting, we are all just like a great family – and one whose membership enriches all. Whoever heard of a family that didn't have its share of squabbles and disputes; indeed, you could argue that a family that doesn't fall out from time to time has something wrong with it. But the strength of the family lies in its support in good times and bad.

Sometimes, the bad times are made good by the family's intervention, and there are even occasions when the good times are made even better, as with the tale of Elsie and Jack Beecham. The couple were delighted to win the £1,000 Golden Nugget prize draw on Wally Webb's Saturday show, back in the early eighties. The money was to go towards a hoist for Elsie, whose arthritis made climbing stairs very difficult. But she was still short of £600 to complete the purchase and, as the *EDP* reported:

> Within minutes, the couple's winnings were nearly doubled after an appeal on the airwaves brought promises of cash from people throughout Norfolk.
>
> Wally Webb ... said the station had pledged an extra £100 from its Helpline kitty ... and the Norwich City promotions department had promised another £100. The appeal was then broadcast on the air, with

a tremendous response.

'The phones just did not stop ringing,' said Wally. 'The girl on the switchboard was in tears with the offers she was getting.'

He said the £600 target had been met within 20 minutes, and the extra money raised would be added to the Helpline funds.

At least, Jack and Elsie had each other, and, though I won't dwell on it too much, I've often wondered how many of our listeners manage on their own. How many, for that matter, will hear any other voices throughout the entire day except those on the radio? I suspect that even that latter figure is very substantial, and one that more than justifies the special goodbye that Roy Waller always gives at the end of his daily show.

If I want to quote a show that particularly proves the importance of audience participation, I need not look too far. The *Midday* programme is ten years old on 13 November 2005, and, almost from the outset, it has been listener-led. The subjects and issues stem in the main from the letters and calls that come in from the audience. Of course, BBC TVs *That's Life* – and before that, *The Braden Beat* – were detailing consumer complaints more than 20 years ago, but it was still pretty much of a novelty for local radio, back in 1995.

To be honest, even those of us on air did not appreciate what we had on our hands when we first started taking on your problems. Radio Norfolk's Action Desk had just been launched, and we simply handed your queries on to its coordinator, Gary Standley, and his team of volunteers. After resolving the issue, Gary would make a brief appearance to tell the tale from start to finish. Blink and you'd miss him, sandwiched in-between the conventional interviews we ran then with specialists and spokesmen. But the telephone calls poured in and, gradually, we recognised that we were virtually throwing away the most valuable element of the show.

So we changed things around, placed the emphasis on these items and, crucially, began to put the callers on air. When you had 'irate of Itteringham' or 'angry of Ashwellthorpe' pursuing the representative of the organisation that had upset them, things just seemed to get done quicker. There's no doubt that the push comes, too, with the knowledge that it's the BBC behind the enquiry. By now, there must be hundreds of Norfolk listeners who will happily give three rousing cheers for those little letters and the help they've provided. But, in our turn, we in the BBC cheer those hundreds too, because, without them we would not have a show to put on.

It's unfortunate that the problems arise in the first place, of course, but if they do, we need the opportunity to tackle them. So what is the most significant assistance that we have ever provided on the *Midday* show? It is a question I've often mulled over, the real problem being, of course, how to define that word 'significant'? The easiest way would be to put it in financial terms. In that case, I suppose, it has to be the case of the lady who was lumbered with doctors' fees of £11,000, when her husband suffered a stroke abroad. The insurance company claimed that, since he was over 80 at the time of the stroke, the policy was no longer valid. But, after we pointed out that the insurers had not identified any age limit when he had renewed the policy the year before, they reluctantly coughed up.

Action man: Gary Standley

What about the personally significant? This is much more difficult to select, but if any one story deserves to be repeated, it has to be the case of the bereaved grandmother. Even coming on air must have been enormously traumatic for the woman concerned, because her daughter had just died after being involved in a car crash. With exceptional bravery, she overcame her grief to make an appeal on behalf of her grandson, as he languished in hospital. The little boy had been in the back of the car and, although his injuries were relatively light, his very new top-of-the-range model car had been crushed. For a 6- or 7-year-old who had still to be told what

29

had happened to his mother, this was one of the worst things imaginable. But, despite her most strenuous efforts, Grandma hadn't been able to find another one anywhere. Could we help – which really meant of course, could you help?

Now, when there are a large number of possible outlets to be checked, our 'internet of Norfolk' often proves invaluable, but, on this occasion, even your efforts failed. It soon emerged that this particular model car had proved so popular that there was not a single toyshop, not just in Norfolk, but throughout the country, that had any cars in stock. If we wanted to order from the United States, that was a possibility; but in that case, we might have to wait days or even weeks for the model car to be despatched. It left us in a quandary, because this little boy's need was now.

I should not have worried. There is always someone who comes up with a solution and, on this occasion, the someone was a firm friend of the programme – and a generous one to boot! I will not embarrass him by quoting his full name, but 'Jim' and 'Weybourne' aren't a million miles from the mark. What he did was to break through the artificial barriers that we, in our innocence, had erected, by putting himself in the child's place. He recognised that, while we were obsessive over the idea of an exact replacement, to a 6 or 7-year-old, just as long as a present is adequate to the task, it will always be welcome.

Only a day or two later a box arrived in our office with instructions to get it to Grandma as soon as possible. Inside was another model car from the same range – not the same model, of course, but very similar. We sent it off, asking her to report back. So, did the child mind that it wasn't precisely the same? Not at all.

When it comes to stories that grab the headlines, it's the quirky ones that take precedence. I am tempted to say they're usually the ones that really do not add up to a can of beans, but that would be to insult the many – and I mean many – who helped our man Keith Greentree in doing precisely that – adding up the beans in a can! Says Keith:

> It was about six years ago now and all I did was to
> muse on air about the number of baked beans there

might be in the average can. This stemmed from a quiz question I'd posed, namely, 'What do Britons get through 185 million of in the course of a year?' Now my book's answer was 'cups of tea', but Michael from Attleborough was convinced that it was baked beans instead. When I challenged him to prove it, he went away and counted the contents of one tin from his cupboard. From this, he argued, we could establish the total number of individual beans by multiplying his figure by the total number of cans sold.

QUEST ■ Supermarket rivals reveal baked bean secrets

Listeners lift lid on the great bean mystery

Picture: FREELANCE

A disc-jockey started a counting craze when he jokingly mused on air about how many baked beans there were in the average can.

Scores of listeners immediately began opening tins of baked beans and painstakingly counting them. But the apparently pointless exercise soon revealed there were a lot more baked beans in some tins than others.

DJ Keith Greentree, 59, compiled a baked bean "hit parade" from his snap sample. The volume of callers showed it was a genuine consumer issue, said Keith.

The survey revealed, for instance, that a can from a Somerfield supermarket had 200 more beans in it than rivals, providing extra mouthfuls for bean lovers.

Mr Greentree, a DJ for BBC Radio Norfolk, said listeners had gone to considerable trouble to get their final bean totals correct.

"It all started when I asked on air what Britons get through 185 million of every day," he said. "The actual answer was cups of tea, but this chap phoned up - "Michael from Attleborough" - and said he thought the answer was baked beans. I asked him how on earth he knew how many beans people ate.

"Ten minutes later he phoned up again and said he had counted how many beans were in his tin and there were 442. I then mused on air about whether it was the same number in every can and people started phoning up saying they had counted them. There were scores of people phoning up and it really seemed to capture the imagination.

"It seems a bit bizarre but I think it shows where people are getting value for money."

Mr Greentree says the bean count is over after callers phoned in their totals over four days.

Beans in a standard, 420g tin

IN THE CAN: Radio Norfolk DJ Keith Greentree.

were as follows: Co-op 382; Sainsbury 419; Heinz 419; Tesco - samples of 422 and 440; HP 442; Lockwoods 495; Somerfield 642.

Mr Greentree pointed out the Co-op tin had cost just 11p.

Somerfield head of corporate affairs Jill Rawlins said its Italian-grown beans had perfect curves. "There is no specific reason why we have more beans in our tins. We just cram in more," she said. "Our beans don't have to swim around lonely in the tomato sauce looking for friends."

Tesco spokesman Mr Russell Craig revealed the trade secret over why some cans have more baked beans than others.

"Believe it or not there is legislation for baked bean producers on the quality, size, and number of the beans in cans," he said. "Every 30 minutes there are quality control checks on baked bean production lines.

"The reason there are discrepancies is because the production line uses something called a volumetric filler and that is adjusted according to the size of the beans.

"The reason there were more beans in the Somerfield can is because the beans were smaller."

So there you have it.

Source:
Eastern Daily Press

Well, I forgot about opening cans of worms, for before I knew where I was, scores of listeners were opening cans of beans and counting their contents. Needless to say, different cans contained different totals, which then led to the most bizarre of hit parades ever. Top of the crops turned out to be Somerfield 420-gramme tins, with a mighty 642 beans, compared with the 'lowedy from the Co-op', with only 382.

But it wasn't just Radio Norfolk's listeners who got full of beans over this, most of the popular press took up the 'bean-a-thon' too, leading, among other things, to my photo sharing page 3 of *The Sun* – which was nice!

Unfortunately, the budget for this book didn't stretch to permit us to include the page 3 in question, but it does provide a rather nice symmetry to those contents of this chapter, starting as we did with those naked travellers in Norwich. And it proves beyond doubt that, with your help, it's not just the *News of the World* that can boast that 'all human life is here'.

Where are they now?
Phil Johnson

I joined Radio Norfolk at the very start – I *am* one of the originals. I even arranged to get married in the summer before the station opened, as I did not want to miss it. I was working at BBC East as a station assistant on the old Radio 4 regional programme called *Roundabout East Anglia* with John Mountford. I was a trainee, having recently left university.

My early memories are of Roy Waller being an AA man, David Clayton being an entertainment agency boss who came in and did programmes, and dear old Ron Fielder walking in late one night, his face masked with dust from harvesting, determined to get his farming chat recorded.

I think I did everything – I started by going out on Saturday mornings in the radio car for the *Ian Masters' Show*. We used to have a password – something like 'soggy sausages' – and people would rush out when they saw us, shout the password and get on the radio. I have presented every single part of the output at various times; the most difficult was when I was sports editor for three months doing *Saturday Special*. It was a nightmare, as I just knew so little about football. I ended up presenting the breakfast show, and then being a news producer until I went into television.

I once persuaded a Euro MP to join me in an April Fool spoof that the European wine lake was going to be stored in Hickling Broad, and that wine would come out of people's taps – red wine from 'hot' and white wine from 'cold'. Great moments for me were interviewing Michael Palin and Spike Milligan, plus the Radio Norfolk holidays and especially the trip to Belgium when we took over an entire deck on a ferry. We decided to run a disco and nearly blew the electrics on the whole ship.

I left in 1985 and joined *Look East*, where I was a reporter, newsreader and assistant news editor. In 1990 I joined Anglia Television to do similar things and in recent years I've been producing and presenting documentaries. My daughter, Nicola Stonehouse, is keeping the family tradition going and is working on BBC Radio Cambridgeshire.

Where are they now?
Neil Walker

Before Radio Norfolk went on air in 1980, we did a dry run at the Royal Norfolk Show. My hands were shaking so much the needle skidded straight across the record. Luckily thunder and lightning intervened, and we had to shut up shop for safety reasons. As a dyed-in-the-wool journalist and not a DJ, I never really did get the hang of it. Producer Bob Ledwidge dubbed me the 'king of approximate broadcasting'. Fair enough.

Partnering David Clayton on the *Norfolk Airline* morning show was the happiest time of my entire working life. We were lucky that the manager, Keith Salmon, gave us a completely free hand – though he did come and scowl at us through the studio window when I suggested we should see more men's willies on billboards to even up the sexual stereotyping! We had a simple philosophy – no subject was barred unless it was boring. Great interviews were allowed to run. Dull ones were cut short. Reading the funnies out of *The Sun* was more likely to please the listener (and us) than talking about the council tax. I now watch successful daytime network television shows, like *Richard and Judy*, and reflect on how similar they are to the *Airline* format.

Circling the airwaves: guests on Airline

Winning a Sony Radio Award in 1986 propelled us both into network radio. I then worked for Radio 4 as a freelance presenter and producer until I formed my own production company in 1990, making feature programmes for Radio 4, Radio 2 and the BBC World Service. Being invited to help South African radio prepare coverage of its first free elections in 1994 was the most demanding and exciting two months of my career, especially when polling lasted, not 24 hours as expected, but a gruelling seven days! Seeing a legless man being transported to a polling station in a wheelbarrow means I will never fail to cast my vote.

Radio journalism gave me a wonderful life, but as I approached 50 I could not see any great new challenges on the horizon. Rather than get stale and feel frustrated, I decided to give it up completely and start something new. Now my wife Judith and I run a modest property development company, which allows us to work as much or as little as we choose, as well as to travel a great deal. But I do miss my radio work and look back with very fond memories to those crazy Radio Norfolk days.

Chapter 3

The news desk
Jill Bennett

There is an old saying that journalism is history in a hurry. When you look back at 25 years of BBC Radio Norfolk's gathering of the news and occasionally of making the news, you find it has become part of the warp and weft of Norfolk's own history.

In 1980 we were an unknown quantity. People were used to telling the newspapers about the events and issues of the day, but local radio was an innovation. All through the summer of that year, the Radio Norfolk team was busy spreading the word about the new radio news service. Local police, councillors, officials and well known community figures were encouraging, but some were slightly alarmed when it came to talking into a microphone, or venturing into our studios at Norfolk Tower. I recall one MP vowing he would never do any interviews before 10 am, because that was when he had breakfast. If we wished to ask him questions, it would have to wait until later in the day!

We were an innovation, too, because all the producers and reporters were involved both with the programmes and the news. So for some of us, it was a question of getting to grips with radio; for others who had been in radio for a while, it was a question of getting to grips with journalism. We were breaking new ground, and we were full of ideas and enthusiasm. We carried the principles of BBC news: accuracy, fairness, quality, originality. But in technology we were trying out new ways of working.

Right from the start, newsreaders not only gathered, wrote and recorded news and news interviews, but also 'drove' the bulletins themselves, using tape cartridges rather than reel-to-reel tapes to play in audio reports or clips. This meant that only one person was needed in the studio. Previously, on old local stations, an assistant had had to be there to play in the audio when required.

The national news came on teleprinters in a ready-made

hourly format, known as the rip 'n' read. In theory, you could tear the paper off the printer, walk straight into a studio and read it, but this was to risk the vagaries of technology, as it existed then. Sometimes a story would start logically, and then end in a series of question marks and asterisks or other mumbo-jumbo. Sometimes it would stop in mid-sentence. Sometimes a word or two would be missing, leaving you wondering what *should* be there. And sometimes, when it did not arrive until a minute or two after the hour, a bulletin would have to be assembled hastily from material sent earlier.

Our local news, written on heavy old Adler typewriters, was always mixed with the national and international stories. We set out to tell the news of the day, judging its importance or interest to the people of Norfolk. That meant a major local story could lead the bulletin, without our listeners' being kept waiting to hear it. Some of the more traditional stations regarded this as heresy.

At the time the opening day was looming, the news team searched for a good story to lead off our coverage. It turned out to be that the long-established engineering firm of Laurence, Scott and Electromotors in Norwich was changing hands. This was a major employer in Norwich, and it was about to be bought by a company called Mining Supplies. Later the business was to change hands again, this time being bought by FKI.

The news over those first few years often returned to the changing face of Norfolk industry. The Norvic shoe factory, the biggest and most modern in the country at the time, closed down and was sold off. We traced the ventures started by some of its former workers and covered the sale of the factory and its contents. This was a taste of what was to come for many companies in the Norwich shoe industry, and for the thousands of highly skilled men and women who worked for them.

Metamec of Dereham closed down after many years as one of the country's biggest clockmakers, Boulton and Paul moved its main manufacturing base away from Norwich and Crane Fruehauf closed its large North Walsham trailer-making factory. In King's Lynn, the valve-makers Bespak were growing and strengthening their position; and we tracked the progress of firms like Porvair and Dow Chemicals.

Then there was farming, always a feature of our early-morning breakfast shows. Ron Fielder, who farmed at Salhouse, kept us in touch with one of Norfolk's biggest industries. On Royal Norfolk Show days he was in his element. I can remember driving him round the showground in the early morning, as the stockmen and women were getting their animals ready for showing.

'I think we'll have a look at the goats,' Ron declared, striding off towards their pens.
A woman was just walking back with two goats.
'Ah,' he cried, 'we'll talk to this lady.'
She stopped for us and Ron waited for the programme to hand over to him. As soon as he was live, he boomed an introduction to the goat owner and floored her completely with his first question, 'Have you been sleeping with your goats, m' dear?'

Country living: Ron Fielder, Charles Henderson, Simon Mcfarlane and Ray Loose

The Norfolk countryside has taken an important part in the news throughout all of our 25 years. Local efforts to keep the unique grazing marshes of the Broads area from being deep drained and ploughed finally reached the House of Commons, and ended in a new scheme being announced in 1985. The controversy brought the then environment secretary, Michael Heseltine, to Acle village hall to address more than 200 farmers from the area. It also brought our microphones, as the story was not just local but national, because of the importance of the Broads as a wildlife area.

The debate over coastal sea defences began: Professor Keith Clayton, from the University of East Anglia, held that trying to stop the sea gnawing away our coastline was futile and expensive. Householders and landowners living in those areas took a different view. We interviewed successive ministers who came to view the issue first hand. Also, on many stormy winter nights, we would be on flood watch: chasing the high tide round the coast as it threatened homes and farmland with flooding, getting the most up-to-date reports from our own reporters and from the flood defence engineers.

One of the most memorable nights was in 1993 when, not only was there a high tide, but an engineering barge broke loose and careered through Cromer Pier. Wally Webb was the man on the spot with the radio car, watching as the drama unfolded. I was in the newsroom, updating the flood news every half-hour. With the wind howling round him, Wally watched as the middle section of the pier was demolished, leaving the lifeboat shed cut off.

Wally Webb braving the elements with the radio car

When natural disaster strikes, the Radio Norfolk newsroom is more than a gatherer of stories. The priority is getting the relevant information to people in the county, whether it is issuing a flood warning, or dealing with the effects of bad winter weather, when snow or freezing temperatures lead to school closures and problems on the roads. At times like these, the newsroom is helping to get the news out as it happens.

In our early days, we had several hard winters, when Norfolk was brought to a standstill by several feet of driven snow. Roads were blocked, villages cut off for days and power supplies disrupted. We had reporters out in Land Rovers helping to get food through to some villages. During the worst of those winters, Stephen Cape, one of the BBC's national correspondents, came to lend a hand because he couldn't get to London to work. He set off with a fuel tanker that was trying to reach an old people's home in Mundesley, where heating oil was running perilously low. It was a day-long cliff-hanger, as they had to contend with snowdrifts and cars stuck on the roads, as well as the dreadful weather conditions. Stephen reported back to us and to national radio as the tanker made its way north, with a dramatic blow-by-blow account. They got through in the end – I think everyone cheered.

The hurricane that swept across the county in 1987 was even more dramatic. It brought a huge amount of damage and mayhem. Throughout that morning, we heard warnings that you should not go out unless absolutely necessary. The exception was the schools: the Norfolk education service was sticking to its policy of saying all schools should be open and all pupils should get to them. In the end, I rang the county education officer, who was apparently in the shower, and asked if the authority could at least soften the line, so that children didn't have to brave the chaotic and dangerous conditions outside. He skilfully found a form of words that didn't offend county policy, but enabled kids to stay in safety at home.

Politics, both local and national, have always been an important part of our output. One of the biggest challenges is to cover elections. Our first taste of that was the 1981 Norfolk County Council election; we've done every one since. It's an exercise that involves everyone: reporters at every count, aided and abetted by someone to help take down results and find guests. It means booking broadcast lines, visiting all the places where counts are taking place to make sure we can get into the buildings, hiring phone lines and extra help, and getting the paperwork organised for the studio presenter and guests.

We cast around, that first time, for experts to interpret the night's results as they came in. John Greenaway, from the University of East Anglia, became our resident commentator to share the long evenings of broadcasting, as the shape of county or district councils changed or when our MPs were up for election. By the time the overnight team finished the job of live broadcasting, and then reports for the morning audience, dawn would be breaking outside Norfolk Tower and our resident car-park blackbird would be singing his morning greeting.

Many national politicians came through our doors: cabinet ministers, opposition spokesmen and – women; they came to make their bids for support at the ballot box. There were times in-between, too, when they would come to talk about the issues of the day and field questions from Radio Norfolk listeners. On one of those occasions, Jim Prior, then the Northern Ireland Secretary and Waveney MP, reflected that he had done all he could in the job. It was a statement that made immediate headlines in our bulletins and via the BBC across the world. Radio Norfolk was even mentioned on the front page of a paper in Japan.

Howard's way: Tony Mallion interviews former Home Secretary

Sometimes international events make our local headlines. We have followed the fortunes of our armed forces through the Falklands War, the two Gulf wars and the conflict in Kosovo. As home to two important RAF stations, we have been more closely involved than many areas.

41

All through the years, we have been part of recording Norfolk's celebrations. Many have been royal occasions. Remember the Queen coming to Norwich Cathedral in 1996 to distribute the Royal Maundy? Then there was the 75th anniversary of the Royal Air Force, marked as a major national event at RAF Marham; Prince Charles visiting Caister lifeboat; the Queen Mother at the Sandringham Flower Show – Radio Norfolk has been there for literally hundreds of royal visits, to enable everyone to share them. Successive reporters have had to decide how to describe the colour of an outfit and maybe the hat as well, often having to commentate on a visit live, via the radio car.

Usually, a royal story is all about celebration, but the death of Diana, Princess of Wales, put the whole country in mourning, not least of all Norfolk, where she'd grown up on the Sandringham Estate. There was a sense of personal loss, too, with the death of the Queen Mother, who loved the royal estate and the life of West Norfolk, helping the King's Lynn Festival to thrive. Many individual memories were shared through the Radio Norfolk airwaves.

There have been so many stories – the story of Norfolk, told as it happens. In the 1980s, it seemed we spent a great deal of time reporting on the opening of roads and the closing of schools, on huge new developments, like the building of the Castle Mall, and on the seemingly endless debates about Great Yarmouth's bid for an outer harbour and the merits of a new hospital for Norwich. Now some of this is history, some still carries on.

Flying high: Jill Bennett reporting from the Hardwick flyover

As technology has progressed, so our capabilities have increased. In the late eighties, a new linked computer system enabled us to exchange information with other stations without having to spend hours on the phone taking down copy from elsewhere. The ubiquitous Uher reel-to-reel tape recorder, the workhorse of the newsroom, has been succeeded by new formats in recent years, but for the best part of two decades it was the mainstay of the newsroom. Editing was with razor blade and sticky tape: a real art.

Technical improvements have also brought changes in the way programmes sound. News and current affairs programmes in the early days were a mix of music, news and current affairs. Our first breakfast shows, presented by John Mountford, ran through to 10 am, and included music, dedications, a what's on diary and features. At 10, we joined Radio 2, but on the hour we would opt out again to read our own local news bulletins. It was something of a challenge, reading a three-minute bulletin with the Radio 2 bulletin in one ear and our own in the other, having to finish at precisely the same moment as Radio 2 and re-introduce the Jimmy Young programme, going back to it at the moment the first disc played.

Gradually we introduced more speech and more guests. The programme was shortened as we introduced the *Norfolk Airline* mid-morning. Later, a short drivetime programme appeared for the first time, bringing an update on the day's events, and finally the mid-afternoon carried a Norfolk programme as well. By the time the BBC decreed we should have even more speech output, we had already had a few months with a lunchtime news and current affairs programme.

Now the style is more relaxed, but Radio Norfolk has never been very formal. Somehow, sharing the news with friends and neighbours isn't the occasion for being too starchy – and when it's live radio there's always the possibility of a hitch of some kind.

Where are they now?
Carol Bundock

I was born in Redhill in Surrey, but later moved to Norfolk and have spent my entire broadcasting career in the county. I joined Radio Norfolk in 1989, just after graduating from the University of East Anglia with a degree in Drama and English. Within six months I was presenting the flagship breakfast programme, *Today in Norfolk*, which I did for two-and-a-half years. Apart from having to be at work at 5 am every day, I thoroughly enjoyed that time. I met and interviewed many of the movers and shakers in Norfolk, and loved the buzz of being able to get breaking stories on air in seconds.

I then went on to present a two-hour morning programme – my brief from the then station manager, Keith Salmon, was to create a local *Woman's Hour*. I loved this too, and learnt so much from the whole host of guests who appeared on the show.

All presenters make slips. The one I remember happened when, announcing a 'what's on', I inadvertently told the county that at a summer village fête, they would be serving 'tea with fresh cream scouts', instead of scones – ah, the joys of live broadcasting!

After about five years at Radio Norfolk, I moved across the road to television and *Look East*, where I still present and report. But it was local radio that gave me the taste and appetite for broadcasting, and provided me with a career I feel privileged to have. My abiding memories of Radio Norfolk are happy – I worked with some wonderful people, and we shared

Carol with daughter Laura

a real sense of fun and hard work, always wanting to get the stories about our fantastic county out to the people who mattered most, our listeners.

I've lived in Norfolk for 30 years now, and never intend to move. Both my children were born here, and my son Jonathan works locally as a tree surgeon. My daughter Laura has followed me into journalism and is at present working at the BBC Television Centre in London for *Breakfast News*. My partner, Ian, is in the business too. We live in Thorpe St Andrew, with two dogs, and enjoy gardening, cooking and entertaining. I'm also honoured to be county president of both Girlguiding Norfolk and the British Red Cross.

Where are they now?
Ian Hyams

Here I am living in America – in Nashua, about 50 miles north of Boston, New Hampshire – and still broadcasting, mostly to various BBC regional and national stations from my home-based studio. Hardly a day passes without my first checking the BBC Norfolk website to find out what's happening in a county where we lived so happily for 30 years.

Just recalling the pleasure of moving out of the BBC's main radio newsroom in London and being the first news editor at Radio Norfolk brings a smile to my face. Escaping the world of international news to a county which welcomed our coverage of local issues, made us all feel like local heroes.

Voice of America: Ian Hyams reports

It was such fun; from meeting the extended listening public at the Royal Norfolk Show to the visitors who regularly dropped in to our Surrey Street studios. It was an experience that I still gain from today as I put on my headphones, face the microphone and talk to perhaps millions of listeners, yet concentrate (as professional broadcasters should do) on chatting to just one person – like I used to with you.

Chapter 4
The library burns, a princess dies and Tony Blair comes to town

Sarah Kings

Over the years Radio Norfolk has had its share of big stories but, despite being a news editor, I have to make a confession – I have an uncanny ability to be nowhere in sight when the big story breaks. Nothing intentional, you understand, just a question of *not* being in the right place at the right time.

When the Central Library caught fire in Norwich in the summer of 1994, I was heading out of the county for a family holiday in the Lake District. As we approached Norwich, I noticed a huge plume of smoke over the city.

'That looks like a big fire to me, stick the radio on,' I said to my husband, only moments after declaring the holiday a news-free zone.

Jim Cassidy: hot news

We were just in time to hear presenter Jim Cassidy say reports were coming in of a big fire at the library. Over the next hour, the enormity of the situation became apparent as firefighters battled, without success, to save the building and its precious contents.

Jim Cassidy recalled how the news broke in the newsroom that day:

We received a call from Norfolk Police to say that Bethel Street was closed because of a fire. When we checked with the fire service, we were told they were fighting a blaze at the library. David Line was my producer that morning and we decided to take Matthew Gudgin off the sports bulletins to take the radio car down and report live from the scene. Little did we know at that time, the fire would lead to the destruction of the building.

At nine o'clock, the early morning team normally went for breakfast in the BBC canteen, but that morning, as we walked out of Norfolk Tower, a huge pall of smoke hung over the city. We decided to go along to the market for a bacon butty and a cup of tea. We stood, along with scores of people, watching as firefighters, drafted in from around the county, tried in vain to save the library.

Source: Eastern Daily Press   *Summer of 94: Norwich library ablaze*

It was a tragedy for Norfolk, though, of course, without that fire we would not be in the magnificent Forum today. After the fire, we followed the huge rescue effort to save thousands of historical documents. Radio Norfolk was also instrumental in collecting thousands of books for the new library.

Some years later, I was away again for another massive Norfolk story – the shooting of a burglar in Emneth by farmer Tony Martin. I arrived back from holiday a couple of weeks later to find the story was still causing uproar, dominating the bulletins both nationally and locally. It was a story we would end up covering for many months to come.

When Tony Martin was released from prison, I went along with Roy Waller to interview him in a pub out in West Norfolk. It was very strange to finally meet the man whose story I had been following for several years. Despite spending over an hour in his company, I came away none the wiser about who he was and what made him tick.

One of my most memorable pieces of reporting in Norfolk was making a documentary about the 1953 floods. The recollections of an elderly woman at Sea Palling about that terrible January night remain to this day my personal favourite of all my work. Her vivid story of how her house had literally fallen down around her and how she'd put her baby into a wardrobe to float away, in the hope he might be saved, makes the hairs stand up on the back of my neck even today – both were rescued, by the way.

Sometimes we are caught completely off guard. Royal deaths are events that are anticipated and planned for in the BBC, and there is a set procedure across the Corporation for dealing with them. Yet there was nothing that could have prepared us for death of Princess Diana, in the middle of Paris, in the middle of the night. At Norfolk Tower there had been installed a special light which was supposed to flash in the newsroom to indicate a royal death. It failed, so it was fortunate that presenter Gary Standley happened to switch on the television at his home to enable us to get across the story early on, as he recalls:

> For some reason I couldn't sleep very well that night and woke early and turned on the television –

something I normally never do in the morning. I couldn't believe what I was seeing, as reports of the accident involving Princess Diana were just coming through. At that stage Diana was still believed to be alive, but when a little while later I arrived at Radio Norfolk, I could hear the National Anthem playing as I entered the door. I feared the worst.

Christian White

Christian White was one of the reporters called in that day:

Gathered in the newsroom were half-a-dozen or so familiar faces summoned from their beds. Ian Hyams, the veteran weekend newsreader, was the only one who'd expected to be working that morning. Alongside him there was the news editor, David Line, as well as David Clayton and Jim Cassidy. I was pretty much the most junior person there. The reason I'd been brought in was down to the list of Royal contacts I'd compiled a few months before. These ranged from Sandringham press officers to the so-called royal watchers, who loyally turn up to wish the royal family well at Christmas. These were the people we'd be interviewing over the coming days, and within hours I'd sent faxed copies of that list to people all over the BBC.

Radio Norfolk took the Radio 4 output initially, but by mid-morning we took back control and David Clayton was on air. Christian recalls:

The phone lines went crazy almost the moment he went on air, and what followed was two hours of intensely moving personal tributes from Norfolk men and women affected by Diana's life and death. As we moved into the early afternoon, we all assumed that the programmes could get back to normal. It's a sign of how badly you can read a moment, when confronted by a historical event as big as Diana's death. Unlike most news stories, which grow through the day and then at some stage start to diminish again, this one just grew and grew. The story continued to dominate the output for the whole of the next week. Each day we thought life would get back to normal, quickly to realise that it was still the only story people wanted to hear about.

The Norfolk newsroom has always had a reputation throughout BBC local radio as being a friendly place to work. That's not to say it's a doddle to pick up the nuts and bolts of radio. I began at the station in 1990, having worked in local newspapers for over ten years. Finding stories was no problem, but actually getting them to air by recording and editing interviews was another matter entirely. My first few months were spent in a haze, as I tried to get the hang of the equipment. I'd often be found working late into the night surrounded by a sea of quarter-inch tape.

A lot of success in radio is down to bluff, and Graham Barnard confesses that he used bucket-loads of it to land his first reporting assignment at Radio Norfolk:

I have to admit I lied on my first day's work experience when Ian Hyams, that day's news editor, asked me if I knew what I was doing just before I made it to air later that day. I only succeeded with loads of help from producer Debbie Tubby – who to this day has kept secret the fact that I didn't know what I was doing and really shouldn't have been in the newsroom at all.

Debbie Tubby: working lunch

50

A few days later, Graham was in another fine mess, when another producer took him to one side and gave him some friendly advice:

Graham Barnard: don't panic Mr Mainwaring

I was about to interview someone terribly important on the phone. The producer went through the basics of phone interviews: explaining to the interviewee what was happening, at which point the interview would be recorded and that the interview would be edited before transmission, plus, of course planning the actual questions. His advice was to stop for a few minutes, stop panicking and just think about what I was doing.

It was a slightly terrifying experience, but the advice still sticks, and before long I was passing it on to other new boys and girls. That's been the best bit about Radio Norfolk for me. I know it's a cliché, but there's a sense of family about it – everyone helps each other.

Over the years we have had politicians of every persuasion grace our studios. Back in the early 1990s, a bright and breezy young Labour shadow minister came in to do an interview with John Mills on the drivetime programme. The guest's name meant nothing to me, but he seemed friendly enough.

After he'd gone, John Mills said to me, 'Watch that man – he's destined for greater things.'

The young man in question was Tony Blair.

Years later as prime minister, Tony Blair was once again in Norwich. He was here to visit the Norfolk and Norwich Hospital, but it was the day of the Stephen Byers resignation in the 'burying news' row. Our reporter Marilyn Rust was sent along to try for an interview. She was feeling very young and inexperienced in the midst of the media scrum. After much waiting around, and being elbowed aside by other journalists, Marilyn managed to secure an interview, and eventually was shown into a room to see the prime minister:

Marilyn Rust: talk of the 'toon'

Being pretty fresh from journalism school in Cardiff, I was very particular about checking my recording levels, normally saying, 'Can you tell me your name and what you do?' Being a little nervous I found myself asking the question, and only when I was halfway through did I realise what I was saying.

He just smiled and said, 'My name is Tony Blair and I'm, well, I'm the prime minister.'

Happily, Mr Blair seemed more amused than affronted, and went on to give a great interview, including answering a question about the banned subject of Stephen Byers. Afterwards he spotted Marilyn's 'Toon Army' badge on her lapel and said, if he'd known she was a Newcastle supporter, he would have given her twice as long an interview.

Sometimes patience wins the day, but at other times it's sheer brass neck that comes out on top. During Norwich City's 1993 European cup run, Bayern Munich came to the city. Normally the newsroom journalists didn't get involved in sport, but we wanted something for the drivetime programme, so reporter Linda Presley was sent out. Linda was not at all sure about this, as she knew nothing about football or the team in question.

'Don't worry,' I said, 'just get there and ask which one is Franz Beckenbauer and then ask him what he thinks about the match and Norwich.'

The chances of getting anything were fairly remote, but it was worth a try. We couldn't believe it when Linda arrived back later, interview in the can. Linda explained the team had been on the coach on the point of leaving. Determined to get something, she leapt onto the coach, demanding to know which player was Beckenbauer. The bemused Bayern Munich players meekly pointed out their manager, and he answered Linda's questions. When she left the coach, she was besieged by other reporters begging to hear the interview, so they could use the quotes.

As we head into the next 25 years at BBC Radio Norfolk, the newsroom remains friendly and hardworking. Everyone brings something to the job, whether it's a relative beginner, brimming with new ideas, or someone with years of experience and local knowledge.

Where are they now?
David Line

For me 1980 was a bad year – 1981 was better. It was the year when I knocked on the door of Radio Norfolk and asked the then news editor, Ian Hyams, to give me a job. I was offered the chance to try my hand at radio reporting. At that time digital editing – in fact, digital anything – was still a twinkle in Bill Gates' eye. In those days it meant lugging around a massive 'portable' recording machine on shoulder straps, with a battery marginally less heavy than that used to start a tractor. You could spot local radio journalists a mile off, for they all had a substantial list to starboard, even when off duty.

The newsroom of Radio Norfolk in those days offered familiar sights and sounds to anyone who had been apprenticed into newspaper journalism. The din of massed typewriters was muffled only by the clouds of cigarette smoke. Instead of working to a deadline of hours in the world of newspapers – or even weeks in magazine publishing – it was now a deadline of minutes. Within a short space of time, I was on staff and a little later promoted to producer. This meant reading the news and, in my case in those early days, not reading it very well. Fortunately, I was not alone. The words 'helicopter' and 'ombudsman' always conspired to trip me up. The former always came out as 'helihopter', the latter just an incoherent mumble.

Growing confidence and improving skills opened the door to practical jokers. On one occasion a certain colleague entered the studio while I was reading the news, pulled out a cigarette lighter and set fire to my script. It was a simple choice. Either read it very quickly or sub-edit as I read. On another occasion the same miscreant dripped water over my head throughout an entire news bulletin. While I managed not to laugh, I was soon to discover that revenge is a very sweet dish best eaten cold. It's very difficult to keep a straight face when someone is mooning at you on the other side of the studio glass partition!

After nearly 20 years with Radio Norfolk, given a few disappearing acts to the BBC World Service and the BBC in the Channel Islands and Essex, it was time to achieve an ambition of 30 years – to live in France. Having seen in the Millennium at Radio Norfolk and later broadcast from my favourite Norfolk steam museum at Strumpshaw Hall, I finally hung up my microphone and took early retirement. By October 2000 my wife and I were ensconced in a 300-year-old farmhouse in the heart of France with four years of solid renovation work ahead, a railway to build, articles to write for an English-language French newspaper, a gîte to run, and a cross-stitch design business to help manage. No, not exactly retirement.

World service: David Line now strums in France

Thanks to the internet, I can still tune into Radio Norfolk from time to time to hear voices both familiar and unfamiliar. So, do I miss the buzz of a radio newsroom, the adrenaline rush just before presenting a programme, the cut-and-thrust of a management meeting, the planning headaches of an outside broadcast? Not on your life!

Chapter 5
Life in the studios
Graham Barnard

I s there anywhere more exciting than broadcast studios? They are at the sharp end of BBC Radio Norfolk, where all our hopes and ideas of what makes great radio finally make it to air. You might think that one studio is no different from the next but, just like the people who sit in front of the microphones, each studio takes on its own special character and personality.

If they are honest, most presenters will admit to having a preference. For example, at Norfolk Tower, I always felt more at home in Studio 1B, even though Studio 1A was lighter and brighter. 1B somehow felt like a good place to learn all the tricks of the trade, maybe because it seemed easier to hide away there. Neither studio at the tower had an outside window; a throwback to the days when it was felt BBC local radio stations should be heard but not seen. How different that view is today? The result is the wow-factor that is The Forum in Norwich. Completing the studio line-up for any local BBC radio station is the NPA, standing for the news production area – posh talk for the news booth.

Old technology: Studio 1A at Norfolk Tower

Someone did once explain to me why each local radio station's studios were always called 1A and 1B. It is something to do with a BBC naming convention that seemed quite dull at the time, and I have since forgotten. But, given that the equivalent studios at The Forum are called 1 and 2, that

Studio 1B at Norfolk Tower

convention seems to be no more. Studio 1 is the larger of the two, as 1A was at Norfolk Tower. This temple of broadcasting boasts the often-mentioned view across the skyline of Norwich. Sandwiched between the two studios is what we call the middle studio. This is where phones are answered, the producer or broadcast assistant does their thing – always within sight of the presenter and vice versa – coffee is made, gossip is shared and guests waiting to go on air are perched on the slightly naff orange settee.

So why do we need two studios? The main reason is that if one studio breaks down, a normal service can be resumed very quickly from the other. Having two studios also allows the next presenter the chance to get his or her act together before going to air. That does not always happen – and sometimes, for technical or practical reasons, some presenters have to 'hot seat' with each other. Stephen Bumfrey and Roy Waller do this at 9.00 each weekday morning, and it is amazing what can be achieved during a three-minute news bulletin. Otherwise, it is a case of studio ping-pong for much of the day, with Wally Webb's 4 am show broadcast from studio 2, with Stephen and Roy in studio 1, John Mills in 2 and so on. This little example of 'how things are done' survived the move from Norfolk Tower, where weekday programmes always started in studio 1B.

Just about everything you hear on BBC Radio Norfolk comes from one of the main studios at The Forum, even if it is an outside broadcast or news bulletin. One of the control main desks will always be 'live', meaning the sound you are hearing is being sent through it before being relayed to the transmitters.

Near-round-the-clock broadcasting means daily life in the studios starts very early in the morning, often a good half-hour before the Radio Norfolk day begins. Wally Webb's flask usually hits the desk in studio 2 at 3.30 in the morning, where the subdued lighting is usually accompanied by a chill, as the air-conditioning unit has had several hours to catch up with itself overnight. There Wally sits, pretty much on his own for the whole three hours, until a cast of thousands, known as Stephen Bumfrey and the *Today in Norfolk* team, arrive at around 6.45 in the morning.

It is then that the calmness and solitude of the middle studio is replaced by the hustle and bustle that accompanies a two-hour all-speech news magazine show. Guests on the breakfast show range from painters to politicians, each waiting their turn in the middle studio. So even by 7 am the atmosphere has changed – the lights go on, and the *flagship* studio gears up to host the *flagship* programme of the day. Then for the rest of the day, the studio complex at The Forum somehow manages to mirror the character of the people who are working there or just passing through. They may each just be four walls, but somehow the studios know what is required of them, adopting the radio-guise of whatever subject matter, be it just on Radio Norfolk, or across the Eastern counties.

Some say you never feel alone in a studio, even if it is not actually live. Broadcast assistant, David Webster, says when the phone lines light up he feels he could be in a room full of a thousand people. The studios seem to keep him company, as he explains:

> "I've spent many a long hour sat almost in darkness by myself answering calls for the Keith Skues show. I never feel alone, as the thoughts of so many people listening to the show seem to beam themselves into the middle studio. It can be so intimate, even though Keith's broadcasting across such a huge area."

For me, the most extreme change of studio gear came on a Saturday night at Norfolk Tower when Paul Barnes transformed studio 1 into something resembling a cabaret club for his '*Gold for Grownups*' show. All he did was switch off all

Tie me down, sport: Rolf Harris playing his digeridoo to producer Simon Ellis

Magic moment: Paul Daniels

Keith Harris and Orville: flying in

No rocking chair in studio for Val Doonican

A touch of Klass and Roy

the lights, working solely by the glow of the controls and a single desk lamp. There was no smoke, but a smoky atmosphere. If you looked hard enough you would often see the likes of Nina Simone belting out a classic number in the far corner – not really, of course, it was just a sorry-looking plant that nobody ever watered.

Wally Webb talking to the County

Even though we have two of them, studio time comes at a premium. There is usually someone doing something in our studios, at most times of the day and late night. There is a booking system, which sometimes works, allowing anyone to reserve time in the studio not being used on air. Some presenters and producers have been known to book studios weeks in advance to make sure they get their precious slot. In the years BC (before computers) reporters for *Today in Norfolk* would often burn the midnight oil while trying to perfect their three-and-a-half-minute report for the following morning's show.

How I remember the clock on the wall of studio 1B at Norfolk Tower telling me to go home, as it was now 2 am. Most reporters and presenters have spent hour after hour locked away in a studio. Producer Nicky Barnes remembers beavering away on some of the old-style equipment at Norfolk Tower:

"One thing that sticks in my mind is editing on reel-to-reel tape and being so indecisive, I used to end up with yards and yards of tape round my neck – just in case I wanted to put that bit of audio back in again! There was something so satisfying about cutting tape with a brand new razor blade, marking it with a newly sharpened china-graph pencil, and sticking yellow leader tape on the front and red leader on the end. Those razor blades were also great to use when decorating – perfect for scraping off surplus paint when you'd painted the windows!"

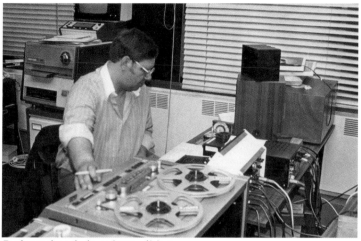

Reel to reel: early days of tape editing

Studio technology has come on by leaps and bounds since the days of cutting and splicing magnetic tape. These days just about everything, including John Mills, is computerised, which means the presenter's control desk now looks very different. At Norfolk Tower, studios 1A and 1B had what the BBC lovingly called 'Mark III' desks: part telephone-exchange, part railway signal-box, part NASA mission control. There was a fader – a knob which controls the sound level for whatever is being passed through it – for pretty much everything, and each fader did the job it was designed to do. For example, the red microphone always appeared on the red fader, the green

Engineer Bruce Roberts unplugged

on the green and so on. In those days, record players, CD players, and various types of tape machine were all connected to the desks, and as technology moved on, more and more shelves with strips of Velcro were fashioned to house the new equipment.

Ground control: our early flight deck

The mechanical desks were built to last forever, and most actions were accompanied by a satisfying clunk. Nowadays, the clunk has been replaced by a click, as computers rule. If you really wanted, you could have the red microphone on the blue fader – but why would you want to? There are no tape machines any more; we rarely play music from CDs or records, although there are CD machines and a record player present. Instead there are six flat computer screens to glare at, a central control console with a big yellow button marked 'GO', a keyboard and 12 faders, all neatly laid out. They say less is more, but while the modern minimalist look would go down well in any Swedish home, somehow I miss the old 'flight deck', which always impressed visitors, who thought it looked too difficult to operate. Station editor, David Clayton, has fond memories of those old beasts too:

> "When the studios at Norfolk Tower were still new and I'd been entrusted with a Sunday morning show, 1B was my home. It had a smell, not unpleasant, of warmed-up electricity. That's stupid – electricity

doesn't smell – but it was a technical smell of the radio desks. Generally speaking the studios were left powered up all day and switched off at night. So for the early show on Sunday, which I used to do, it meant you had to turn on the mains with a satisfyingly large switch beside the studio, which befitted the importance of energising a radio studio into life."

Even though Amy Barratt is one of our newest presenters, she has been around long enough to know that you need to be able to look a Radio Norfolk studio in the eye, and establish mutual respect. She writes:

"Making the move from the cosy news studio into the domain of presenters, downstairs, was a pretty terrifying step. Presenting *Drive Live* for the first time from studio 2 at The Forum made me literally feel sick with nerves. But once I got a few shows under my belt, I felt quite at home, even though the air-conditioning controls are a complete mystery; my guests either boiled or shivered. Studio 2 seems a lot smaller than studio 1. It's tucked away, and people who come to have a look through the glass always seem to look into studio 1 and completely miss studio 2. I think it's something to do with the light and the fact that studio 1 overlooks the view from The Forum – a reminder of everyone who's out there, listening."

Amy, like all other presenters, will tell you a tale of the so-called anxiety dream she recently had. This is where we dream a little dream of something going horribly wrong just at a bad moment. Mine usually revolves around people with nothing to do with the programme, but who descend upon the studio, refusing to be quiet when the red light goes on.

Journalist Nicky Barnes recalls her most common anxiety dream:

"I have a recurring nightmare of being in the Norfolk Tower news studio with 30 seconds to go to the hour (it's normally midday) and being expected to read a news bulletin – but I have no scripts and no tapes. I try and communicate with the news studio on the intercom and no one hears. I wave and shout at the glass, and I can see everyone in the newsroom, but no one pays attention. The seconds tick closer and closer to the hour and I have a feeling of rising panic which gets worse and worse – and then I wake up."

Fortunately, anxiety dreams are just that, and do not form part of real life in the studio. Nightmares can come pretty close to being a reality though, as journalist and presenter Nicky Price remembers. One morning she and I were working together on a rather special and fabulously expensive edition of *Today in Norfolk*, so no pressure on us, then, to make sure all went to plan. Says Nicky:

When you're in the studio, establishing a live link and then actually speaking to a reporter in Swaffham or Fakenham can sometimes prove to be quite a challenge for the Radio Norfolk equipment. During the Iraq war in 2003, we required our equipment in Norfolk Tower, not only to establish a link up with Kuwait, but also to maintain it for two hours.

A BBC reporter, Joe Campbell, was out in the desert with some of the servicemen from RAF Marham and he was co-presenting *Today in Norfolk* with Graham. I was producing the show at that time and linking up with the desert was problematic, to say the least. Often, we'd just hear sounds of the latest sandstorm, with a faint trace of a reporter talking in the background. On this occasion, I remember trying to call up the high quality phone line – known in the trade as an ISDN line, with ISDN standing for 'It Sometimes Does Nothing' – a good ten minutes before the programme, but it just didn't connect.

Graham, in the hot seat, was totally calm – or appeared so – and was confident that the link would work out. My heart was beating quicker and quicker as the line failed to connect, and the clock ticked ever closer to 7.00. Various thoughts ran through my head, as I wondered what on earth we would do during the next two hours if we couldn't talk to Joe in Kuwait. The clock continued to tick – far too fast for my liking – during the introduction to the programme and I was frantically tapping at the black box of tricks, just willing a voice on another continent to answer my call.

Then, at about 7.05, a little red light appeared, and a voice spoke to us from the Gulf. I triumphantly announced to Graham that our man was in the mess tent and ready to broadcast, and promptly sat down in a heap, so relieved that the programme was underway. But dealing with problems like this are, of course, all part of everyday life in the studio as a programme producer. Two hours later, Norfolk's servicemen in the Gulf were using our airwaves to speak to their families back in the county, and it was a very moving programme. It was also nominated for a prestigious Sony award.

Visitors to Radio Norfolk often comment on how a presenter needs to be able to work the controls while trying to sound intelligent. Being studio-savvy is part of life for the news team. Ever-changing technology means there is always something to learn. The biggest-ever change in studio life came when we moved from the clapped-out Norfolk Tower to the state-of-the-art studios at The Forum, said at the time to be the most modern radio studio in Europe.

Senior journalist Rita Johnson is the champion of coming up with little tips on how pushing button 'A' and then button 'B', if something goes wrong, can often get a newsreader out of a tricky on-air situation. Her tips are often published on bits of paper stuck to the news studio wall. As well as handy hints, all studios seem to attract knick-knacks. In 1A at Norfolk Tower

Handy hints: Rita Johnson

there was the aforementioned plant, a toy television that had a picture of Roy Waller stuck on it, and a picture of the BBC1 test card, which Matthew Gudgin would shove in front of the webcam, so no one could see him broadcasting.

Then there were the strange acts of vandalism in the news studio at Norfolk Tower. In the days before digital editing, the razor blades used for cutting and splicing quarter-inch tape often got used for other purposes, doubtless during frustrating late-night editing moments. So much so, I guess no one really knows the number of times the surrounding fabric on the control desk got replaced, or sealed up using industrial-strength sticky tape.

For a reminder of how Radio Norfolk used to broadcast not so long ago, all you have to do is take a look at our district studios in King's Lynn and Great Yarmouth. They are monuments to how we used to live, with control desks similar to the ones we used. District producers Jill Bennett, in King's Lynn, and Tony Mallion, in Yarmouth, are quite rightly deeply fond of the old equipment, which will probably outlast all of us. The old-style studios in the districts and the new equipment at The Forum may be technically compatible, but it gets a little confusing when a reporter or presenter visits a district studio and is forced once again to use a system they have mostly forgotten. It really is *not* like riding a bike, not least because the faders in the far-flung reaches of the Radio Norfolk empire work the opposite way to those in The Forum!

Presenter Andy Archer is a great fan of newspaper surveys about life. I wonder what the findings would be if someone were to carry out research into how many hours, weeks, months or years of our lives Radio Norfolk folk spent in a studio. Whatever the results, I can promise you one thing. Not a single one of us would say it ever seemed too much.

Where are they now?
Carey Clark

I can still recall getting my first contract with the BBC. I was in a phone-box in Tombland in Norwich talking through a story with the news editor, Ian Hyams. He offered me a three-month contract as a producer, and I've been a BBC lifer ever since. Until that point I had done casual shifts.

My mother had moved to Salthouse on the north Norfolk coast just after I had finished my post-graduate course in radio journalism. Those early days were marked by her racing down to the beach in the morning, where I'd gone for a walk, and waving at me to say Radio Norfolk had just called – I was needed in the newsroom or to cover a fire somewhere.

There are so many memories of those five years. Having my cues thrown back at me by the senior producer, Steve Hardy, mispronouncing a Norwich MP's name all the way through a story, reporting the Great Yarmouth Outer Harbour scheme, dodging paper balls as Malcolm Robertson and Roy Waller played cricket up and down the newsroom in Surrey Street, Norwich City winning the Milk Cup and the parade around the City, Norwich City being relegated the same year, the fire at the stadium, Roy Waller's impersonation of Sir Arthur South.

Norfolk was always assumed to be a quiet patch. It wasn't then. There was a period when the BBC's national general news service desk called us 'shotgun county'. There seemed to be one murder after another – including the dreadful killing of Leonie Keating. As a journalist you have to be toughened up, and there is nothing like having to cold call a family that has suffered tragedy.

I remember a family whose son had been kidnapped in Beirut – I had to go and interview them. Weeks went past and then his body was found in the hills around the Lebanese capital. I was with the family as the call from the Foreign Office came though confirming the body was that of their son. It always amazes me that people want to talk to you in those circumstances.

I once talked to a grandfather whose entire family had died

the night before. Carbon monoxide poisoning, caused by a faulty boiler, had killed his daughter, son-in-law and grandchildren. Only his own wife had survived, I think. The doctor had told them a few days earlier that they probably had flu.

There were also hilarious moments. In the summer on Saturdays I used to go out with the radio car with Angie Nehring to a variety of fêtes, but after a few weeks of this live reporting, we realised that the same fair and stalls were going to the same fêtes as we were, week in and week out. There really are only so many times you can do live skittles on air!

The early news shift was always a delight, as well. I always found the 7.30 headlines a low point. I once totally missed them. To this day I have never admitted to Wally Webb it wasn't a technical fault, but my chatting about my latest shopping trip to the breakfast secretary. Phil Johnson would throw in appalling jokes just beforehand, which once made me corpse through the half-hourly headlines.

> Little boy knocks on this man's front door, 'Please, Mister can I have my arrow back?' 'Yes, Johnny. Where is it?'
>
> 'In your cat!'

At that time in the morning anything is funny.

I left Radio Norfolk in 1989 to join the *Today* programme in London. After that I went to television and worked on the *Nine O'Clock News*, News 24, became deputy editor of *Breakfast News*, and am now editor of the BBC World programme, *Hardtalk*. I made so many friends at Radio Norfolk, who have remained friends ever since, and it was the best training any journalist could get.

Where are they now?
Jerry Foulkes

Although I wasn't born in Norfolk, my parents did move to Norwich when I was about three, and I went to Bignold and Earlham schools, so I feel a native. I was also always very keen on radio. At Earlham we started a radio station that broadcast at lunchtimes from a broom cupboard. In the autumn of 1980, just as Radio Norfolk was launching, I went to Leicester University to study geography, and got involved with BBC Radio Leicester, presenting a weekly student and then a new 'youth' programme. They don't have 'youth' programmes now, thank goodness.

The summer before I graduated, my mother told me that the new Radio Norfolk news editor, Ian Hyams, had bought a house down our road, so I went and knocked on his door to ask if I could help out over the summer break. Unfortunately for him, but fortunately for me, it turned out that he had a trainee reporter starting, Helen Fitzgerald, who couldn't drive, so I became her radio-car chauffeur for the summer.

I'm not known for my sense of direction, so my dad asked me how I was finding my way around the county. I told him that I started from Grapes Hill, where there was usually a sign to get me going in the right direction. This has become something of a family joke now, although of course these days the traffic snarls up on Grapes Hill, which is to be avoided at all costs.

When I graduated in 1983, there were two station assistant jobs advertised and I applied for one – not expecting to stand a chance – but it turned out to be the start of four very happy years back in Norfolk. At first my colleague Nick Patrick and I took it in turns to present a Sunday afternoon programme called *Discdrive*, as well as helping to prepare news and sport for the breakfast show and some news reporting duties.

I remember once being sent to make a feature about the RAF Coltishall Search and Rescue Sea King helicopter, which took me out on a training mission on a freezing day in

November. To get in some practice, the crew decided to winch me down onto a sandbank and rescue me. Unfortunately, shortly after depositing me, they got a distress call from a nearby lightship and left me there for about twenty minutes, which on the wintry North Norfolk coast felt more like several hours. When I got back to Norfolk Tower with my portable tape recorder, I thought I would have a great feature, but alas the noise from the helicopter was so loud, it drowned out all the interviews on the tape.

Jerry Foulkes: nightdriver

Finally, after three years of badgering my station manager, Keith Salmon, and the allocation of more money to extend Radio Norfolk's broadcasting hours to 9 pm, in the autumn of 1986, I finally started presenting an evening programme, *Nightdrive*. (It was quickly, and I'm sure affectionately, nicknamed, *Nightdrivel* by Roy Waller.) There were sketches, tracks by local bands and a famous Roy Waller Carrow Road commentary out-take where he was heard to exclaim, 'Look at that! There's a player on the pitch!' which we delighted in running endlessly when he finished his teatime show. There were also competitions where you could win a toothbrush – some years before Chris Evans created a show with a similar theme.

The following year, 1987, I saw an advert in *New Musical Express* looking for video-jockeys for the new pop TV channel MTV Europe. Some students at the UEA who listened to *Nightdrive* helped me make an audition videotape, and after another audition in London I was asked to present a show for six weeks. Peter Glanville, my boss at Radio Norfolk, very kindly let me do *Nightdrive* and MTV for a few weeks, but when MTV wanted me to sign up for six months, I had to leave Radio Norfolk and move to London.

After MTV, I presented the links between the programmes on Children's ITV with a puppet dog, Scally, and then I moved behind the scenes with a string of producing and directing jobs at the BBC, including the World Service and CBBC. By 1996 I became the editor of Channel 4's long-running viewer-access show, *Right to Reply*. Meeting and talking to so many of Radio Norfolk's listeners when I was out in the radio car was a fantastic introduction to meeting so many television viewers.

After a spell commissioning programmes like *Bailiffs*, and *Ground Force* for the BBC, I went back to programme making and my first hit was *How Clean is Your House?* which made Kim and Aggie household names. I helped launch the show in America last summer and co-wrote their best-selling book with all the tips from the TV show. For the last few months I've been sitting in my garden summerhouse writing a book of my own.

I'm still a frequent visitor to Norfolk. My father died last year, but my mother and brother both live in Norwich and we all spend a lot of happy summer days on the beach in Mundesley. I am a very keen gardener and usually leave Norfolk with a bootful of plants for my own tropically themed west London garden, a stone's throw from the famous Ealing film studios.

Chapter 6
The radio car
Wally Webb

The brand-new style of broadcasting introduced by Radio Norfolk marked it apart from national stations. For the broadcasters themselves, it meant a much closer relationship with the audience. You can't get closer than a face-to-face live broadcast situation.

Enter something else that was new to the county: the radio car. Suddenly, out on the open road and in tiny rural communities, this strange vehicle was not just seen but heard. It was a novelty that was also a mobile radio station. Curious onlookers would watch it arrive; minutes later the telescopic mast turned it into a land yacht without the sail. This 'immediate' kind of broadcasting took us straight into the heart and homes of the county, but it did have its limitations.

In that first year of the station I was asked to be the roving reporter every Saturday, an opportunity that I was really pleased to accept. If I have two passions in life they are broadcasting and driving – both in one package? Yes, please.

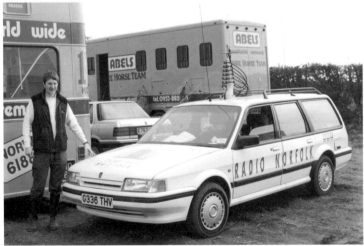

Racing around: engineer Colin Bolton with radio car

Ian Masters was the Saturday morning presenter, and my job was to take the radio car and surprise people. There would be any one of a number of reasons – an anniversary, a village event, a happy ending or a new beginning. Very often I'd turn up unannounced, put up the mast, roll out the cable, knock on the door and go into a home on air to the surprise, delight – and occasionally shock – of the victims. This was broadcasting by the seat of the pants and very exciting.

Then came a new twist. By joining forces with Norwich City Football Club, we made the £1,000 Golden Nugget draw live. Having got the address of the winner, it would be a dash to their home, set up and get ready to broadcast their reaction to the news that they'd won a grand.

Each one was different, but I recall two occasions that were very different from the rest. I would always be accompanied by a representative from the football club, usually Ray Cossey or Mac McKay. In one instance, we approached the front door of a £1,000 winner, cheque in hand. Ian Masters in the studio would be able to 'listen in' in order to know that we were ready and then, at the crucial moment he would put us on air. Now we were live and knocking on the door.

'I can hear someone coming.'

The latch clanked on the door, which, squeakily and very slowly, began to open just a little then stopped. 'Yes.'

'It's Wally Webb and Ray Cossey from the Golden Nugget!'

This was certainly not someone who'd heard the show.

'Who?'

Seizing the moment – this was live radio – Ray drew out the cheque from his pocket and waved it at the face behind the gap in the door.

'Your ticket was drawn this morning and you've won the top prize – one thousand pounds!'

The sight of the cheque was all the stimulus required. A hand instantly grabbed it from Ray's hand and with a 'Thank you very much', just about audible for our microphone, the door was slammed firmly shut.

The second memorable occasion occurred during the first winter, when we sometimes had to set out in very low temperatures. The car handled like most others, taking into account the extra weight of the transmitter equipment. The early models were estate cars, whilst in recent years that's been changed to people carriers, capable of taking the extra equipment we use nowadays and to provide some seating for conducting interviews during really inclement weather.

Previously though, everything had to be done outside the vehicle and the first task on arrival was to raise the mast. The extra height increased the distance we could broadcast, and so the cars have always been fitted with a telescopic 'pole', raised up by an air pump run off the battery. There are six sections to the mast, which are all finely engineered to slide smoothly inside each other.

My mission that Saturday morning was to go to either Taverham or Drayton – and meet listeners in a small cul-de-sac. It was bitterly cold when I put up the mast and made the broadcast. All went well until I tried to lower the mast. The moisture that had run down while the mast was extended had now frozen and made the job of lowering it impossible. No, you can't drive a car with a 30-foot rod sticking out of its roof, although I'm often asked if you can.

It turned out to be a great broadcast, though. Ian Masters regularly returned to us on-air to see how we were doing. We were doing fine. The neighbours had all rallied round.

A touch of frost and radio car mast is stuck

...and finally a listener's hair dryer saves the day

Extension leads had been run from a number of homes and hair dryers came from all quarters, as we slowly melted the ice and the mast came down inch by inch.

Over the years, radio cars have come and gone. The vehicles have improved, the broadcast technology has improved and our broadcast range has increased, so that now we can broadcast from almost all over the county. This happens through receivers that can pick up the signal sent from the radio car, and send it back to the studio via a landline. For example, there's one on the hills overlooking the sea at West Runton, and another at Great Massingham, which enables us to travel farther west.

By far the best improvement, though, has been the use of a radio microphone. This small battery-powered pack enables the broadcaster to be as much as a quarter of a mile from the car, and eliminates the need for a roll-out cable.

When we took charge of our most recent radio car, fitted with this technology, my first job for *Today in Norfolk* was to find people waiting at a bus stop. At the location there was only parking on the opposite side of the road to the stop. Previously I would not have been able to put the cable across a main road, but now I could switch on the radio mic and just walk across and broadcast. This has proved useful in so many different ways. I've had the car on one side of a river and me on the other. I can now be on top of high buildings or deep inside others, where before it would have been too far or too impractical to pull a cable.

So we can now get to you from just about anywhere, and we can be heard broadcasting from the most unusual places. We have been inside an underground reservoir, before it was filled with water, and right to the top of a new multi-storey car park. We have travelled across Halvergate Marshes to the Berney Arms Inn and have taken a train ride and a boat trip, walked along the seashore and even broadcast while riding a tandem.

The daily challenge for me, each morning, is to find my way safely to a chosen location, make sure the interviewees are there and happy, and to get that signal back to Norwich in time for the broadcast. There's the challenge of winter's bad weather and the payback of light warm summer mornings, and there's always the satisfaction of knowing that listeners to BBC Radio Norfolk are being taken to places and hearing the stories live and on the spot.

Patrolling Norfolk: our new car

The radio car equipment
John Adamson

Our first radio car was a Ford Cortina. In the centre of the dashboard was a 15-watt UHF 'link' transmitter. This was a box of electronics about three inches (7.5 cm) tall and 19 inches (48 cm) wide, which generated a broadcast-quality signal to be sent via the aerial on top of the mast back to our studios in Norwich.

Then there was a little three-channel sound mixer. This enabled us to connect a cabled microphone, a Uher (standard-issue portable reel-to-reel tape recorder for pre-recorded interviews) and a radio microphone, which allowed the reporter to broadcast – on a good day – up to 50 yards away from the car.

Below this was the radio telephone, a 25-watt VHF transmitter/receiver, then our only means of communication between car and base. Remember there were no mobile phones in those days, so if we couldn't get a VHF signal from base, the reporter had to run to the nearest phone-box to get in touch with the studio and ask, 'Can you hear me on the link?'

Then there was the car radio, not just for entertainment on the move, for this one was also connected to the reporter's headphones, so he or she could hear the programme when it was time to go live. It was always vital that it was tuned into the correct frequency, or the cue would be missed.

Under the bonnet there was little resemblance to a standard Cortina. With twin compressors for elevating the mast, a huge technical battery to power all the equipment, split-feed alternator for charging the extra battery and a bank of control switches and fuses all squeezed into the engine compartment, it was an unsuspecting mechanic's nightmare.

In the early days, our radio-car coverage was limited to about 15 miles' radius of Norfolk Tower. As time went by and funds became available, we gradually invested in new receiving points in Great Yarmouth, King's Lynn, Great Massingham and West Runton, all linked back to base via landlines. These meant we could broadcast from most parts of the county.

Since these pioneering days of outside broadcasts, our vehicles have become more sophisticated. From Cortina to Montego through Previa to our latest Peugeot 806, each has added extra facilities to allow us to bring more elaborate coverage.

Radio technology has moved on too. Nowadays there is no need for the VHF radio-telephone system to get in touch with base – that has been replaced by a standard mobile phone. The simple radio-microphone, with very limited range, has been replaced by one with a range of several hundred metres. The heavyweight Uher with piles of five-inch tapes – one for every 15 minutes – has given way to a handheld solid-state digital recorder, with a recording time of a whole hour. And gone are the expensive analogue landlines from our receiving points – we now use the cheaper and more reliable ISDN.

But what does the future hold? Mobile-phone technology will soon allow us to send live high-quality sound from a 3G handset, so we will be able to broadcast from anywhere there's a mobile phone signal. And then there are broadband connections and Wi-Fi hot-spots to allow us to hook-up if 3G isn't available. So there will be no need for that power-hungry 15-watt UHF transmitter, the hefty battery, that 30-foot mast and all its control gear – and all those receiving points could be made redundant. In fact, the radio car as we know and love it might well be consigned to history.

Where are they now?
Olly Day

It seems that in one way or another I have always been involved with Radio Norfolk. When the test transmissions first started, I was working down in the cellar of a joke and magic shop in Prince of Wales Road in Norwich, making the stickers and badges for this the latest BBC local radio station. Little did I think then, as I sat amongst the 'crapalot' tea bags and packets of Dr Windbreakers' fart powder, that I would become one of their regular presenters.

I always had a great love of the silver screen, and that was what led me to Radio Norfolk. In 1983, whilst working in Johnny Cleveland's video shop, I was invited by David Clayton to Norfolk Tower to meet his co-host, Neil Walker, with a view to me being a regular guest on the new *Norfolk Airline* programme. It's hard to believe now, with DVDs and cinema being so popular, that this became the very first weekly video review spot on the wireless. Each Friday morning was a hoot, as John Taylor and I laughed our way through the programme, before more fun in the BBC canteen.

This led on to me being offered regular bank holiday Monday specials, which I did for the next ten years. Then Neil and David started the *Airline on Sunday* and I met Freddy Russell, an ageing variety performer who had retired with his accordion to Gorleston. We were thrown together as a team and the 'Ollygrams' were born.

We spent so many happy Sunday mornings travelling round the county surprising people on their wedding anniversaries or birthdays. Nick Gardner would drive the radio car near the house, and we would dash up the garden path singing the victim's favourite songs. This would all happen live on air. Nobody was safe from our roving mike: we jumped out to surprise MPs, OAPs and even some newly-weds in their hotel room – they were still in bed getting their things together!

One of the funniest involved three women staying on a campsite at Reedham Ferry, who were great party-goers and

Back to nature: Olly braves a north easterly

were still drunk at 10 am in the morning. They thought we were from the Salvation Army. The excitement was in tents! 'Not now, Freddy!'

It was like having all my birthdays at once, when I was asked to be the stand-in presenter for Roy Waller on his afternoon teatime show. Sylvie looked after me with the phones, and Heather would pop in with a cuppa. As well as this, I helped out with the presenting on my old mate, Keith Skipper's *Dinnertime* programme. It was a busy but wonderful time of my life.

In the mid-1980s, Peter Glanville offered me a gin and tonic, and a half-hour programme once a week. Stephen Bumfrey was my producer and we started to make the *Olly's Day Out* programmes. We had a great time travelling all over Europe, from the flower markets in Holland to the fish markets in Norway. We even managed to get a full hour out of Belgium. People still ask me about the day I spent with the Cromer fishermen, and the things I saw at the undertakers, not to mention the thing I saw during my day out with naturists!

The last three years at Radio Norfolk saw me opening up my house in Thorpe St Andrew every Sunday morning between 6 and 9 am for *Larks End Radio*. My friends and neighbours would pop in for a chat and a cuppa, Audrey would read one of her *Tat the Cat* stories for the children, and give me a recipe to do each week. Who could forget the outrageous Colin the Milkman, rattling his gold tops as he dropped in for a chat? Even the phone-in competition came from my 'OllyRama' cinema in the upstairs bedroom!

Life is a Cabaret: Olly today

Over the years I made so many friends at Norfolk Tower and met some wonderful people, travelling round the county. Often we would be invited to open a summer fête, with John Fuller and the Radio Norfolk *Roadshow*. The organisers would ask if I would bring my Nanny along, who was then in her 80s, and she loved it. Nanny was a bit like the Queen Mother – she would be asked to judge the Bonny Baby competition or present the prize for the biggest cucumber!

The best thing to come out of my time spent as a minor local celebrity at Radio Norfolk was meeting my future wife, Janet Harnden. Two wonderful children later, I am now as busy as ever performing my cabaret at most of the holiday parks on the East coast and working my magic at special events all over East Anglia, singing at sell-out concerts with the Jonathan Wyatt Big Band and performing on cruise ships round the Mediterranean, Norwich and the Baltic and Caribbean. I have just visited my 600th school in Norfolk with my *Road Safety Magic Show*, which has been seen by over 70,000 children.

Where are they now?
Nick Gardner

I was one of the original 'Wally Webb Gang', set up to present young people's issues on the *Wally Webb Show* on Sunday afternoons, when the station first opened. Phil Johnson recruited me after I interviewed him on Hospital Radio Norwich, where I was a volunteer. I think I was sixteen at the time.

My very first 'on-air' break was provided by Rob Bonnet, who put me in charge of keeping the county of Norfolk fully updated with the latest football scores. It was a bad mistake. Keith Skipper once described my reading of the full-time football results as the most hilarious sound he's ever heard on radio.

Shortly after this I was persuaded to go to university. By graduation in 1985, I was lucky enough to have secured a job back at Radio Norfolk and subsequently stayed for another five

Nick Gardner, g'day sport

years. During this time I worked on everything from the early morning sports bulletins – where my talent for reading the football results was only overshadowed by my mispronunciation of eastern European tennis players' names – to the *Norfolk Airline*, and *Dinnertime* with Keith Skipper.

My most stupid question ever? 'So tell me, how big are bonsai trees in Norfolk?'

The interviewee's answer, 'About 2 to 3 inches.'

I have extremely happy memories of Radio Norfolk, as I was there 'on and off' for ten of my most formative years, and I learnt an incredible amount, not only about broadcasting but about life in general. During that time I met some colourful characters: Eric 'Slasher' Edwards who cut reed at How Hill on the River Ant and whose job, at times, I have coveted, and the Norfolk Spitfire pilot who – on air – recounted the day during the Battle of Britain 'when the Messerschmitts were going down like WAAFs' knickers'.

In 1990 I left for London and the BBC's Television Centre, working at first on *Blue Peter*, as a producer and director, and then as a producer and reporter on *Newsround*, where I covered stories as diverse as the Dunblane tragedy and Richard Branson's global balloon flights. I left the BBC in 1997 and now run my own video-production company.

Whilst at *Newsround*, I met my wife Julie – she sat on the desk opposite me – and we have a little boy called Leo. I keep telling myself when he is old enough to learn to sail on the Broads, I'll have more of an excuse to get 'home'.

Panel game: Aubrey Singer, Mike Chaney and Michael Barton with the Mayor

*A budding broadcaster arrives in reception.
But who is he?*

*Station opening with Terry Wogan,
Mike Chaney and dumpling!*

Press ganged: Keith Skipper launches his latest book with a little help from his Dinnertime Show team

Boarding call: Simon Ellis

Michael Barton maps the future

Legging it: Louise Priest modelling a t-shirt out of the summer range

Philip Nightingale *Angie Eyles* *Dave Penney* *Don Shepherd*

John Fuller *Malcolm Robertson* *Mike Hicks* *Nick Coleman*

Country gents: Tony Mallion and Trevor Austin

Nick Patrick   Peter Pitt   Peter Glanville   Tony Belmont

Simon Ellis   Maggie Secker   Stewart Orr   Bob Ledwidge

Ian Hyams and Peter Glanville broadcasting from a temporary studio in a car park

Birdtalk with Percy Edwards

Noel Edmunds and Wally Webb compare Christmas jumpers

Staff and guests eagerly await the first broadcast from BBC Radio Norfolk

Early Wherry logo

8.52am is no problem for early riser David

The young ones, David Clayton and Wally Webb

Radio Norfolk takes to the air

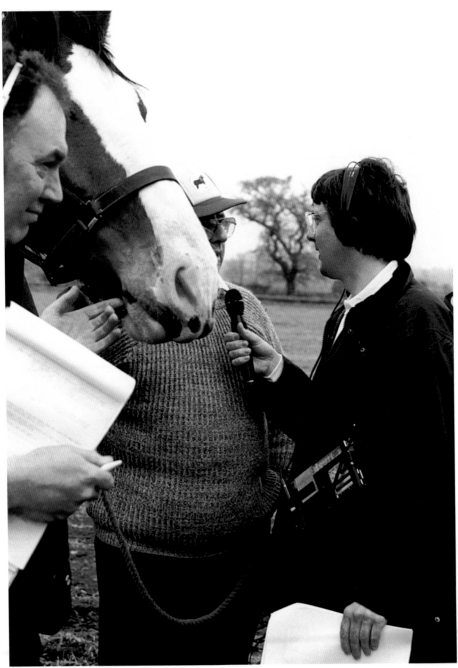

David horsing around

Who is the Skipper on this boat?

On your bike Maggie!

Size isn't everything! David test drives a potential new radio car

Keith noting down where he is on an outside broadcast with Maggie

The boys are back in town, David and Wally on tour

News round Radio Norfolk is that John Craven is in the building

Office politics: Tony Mallion with Leon Brittain

Knowing me, Knowing You – Steve Coogan with Wally

Maggie brewing up a storm with Daniel's fans by giving him a squeeze

Blue Peter making use of our sticky back plastic

Simon Thomas: a walk in the park

Mike Ward cuts the cake to celebrate 10 years of BBC Radio Norfolk

Roadshow to celebrate the 10th birthday of BBC Radio Norfolk

Jill Bennett looking for Mr Darcy

Roy and Sylvie arrive, only to discover that Jill Bennett's outfit looks familiar!

Roy is still disappointed it wasn't a tractor!

Patrick Anthony: mixing it up

Patrick Anthony and Andy Archer cook up a treat for the crowd at the Royal Norfolk Show, watched by co presenter Alison Turpin

David Clayton and Carol Bundock flanked by BBC Radio Norfolk gardeners Charles Henderson and Ray Loose

By Royal appointment, Tony at Sandringham

Antiques expert Mike Hicks and Dinky Toy enthusiast David Cooke offer some advice

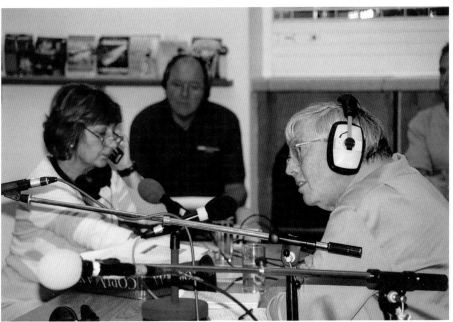

Angie Eyles, Mike Boswell and John Mills take their midday show on the road

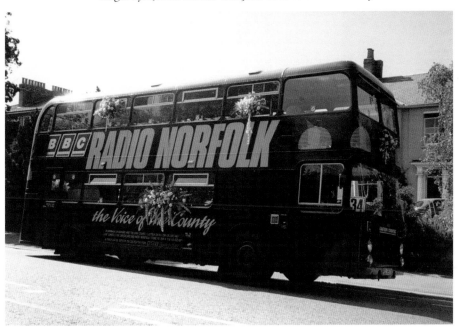

On the buses with BBC Radio Norfolk at the Lord Mayor's procession

CBBC Jake Humphrey with budding TV presenters at the Royal Norfolk Show

Tony Mallion discusses the highlights of the Norfolk and Norwich Festival with Director Marcus Davey

Wish you were here, one of our popular listener holidays

Not far to go now - listeners returning from a BBC Radio Norfolk holiday

Malcom Robertson last day at the station

Norfolk warriors, Olly and David

A night on the Town

Dress down days have started to go a bit too far at BBC Radio Norfolk!

That's the best one I know! David and Neil, Norfolk's very own double act

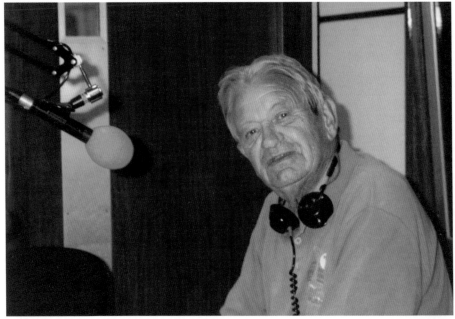

John Taylor preparing for some favourite tunes

Matchday studio at Carrow Road

Are you sure it was a home game this week Neil?

A premier shot, David Clayton and Nigel Worthington celebrating promotion

Just when Neil thought he had escaped Roy's country music in the car at away games!

Roy feeling very blue

Steady on, now's your chance Chris

Graham reflects the end of an era at Norfolk Tower

Receptionist Heather Mills at Norfolk Tower

Gram librarian Cheryl Dilley makes sure all is in order

Celebrating the first day in our new home, The Forum

A room with a view, Stewart settles into his new desk at The Forum

BBC Radio Norfolk Uncovered!

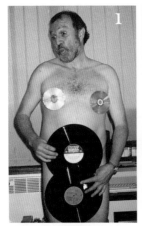

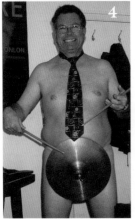

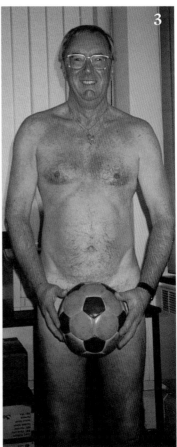

The big events
Tony Mallion

When the merry shout of 'Have you got a 2DB oscillator?' rings out, or, perhaps more ominously, 'Has anyone got a soldering iron?' you can imagine engineers in full cry, as they stretch out long runs of coloured cable, as another BBC Radio Norfolk big event gets under way. These events may be carefully planned for months, or hastily organised in a few hours. Either way they provide another chance to get out and meet the public, create some kind of show or entertainment and, for thousands more, bring one of these happenings right into the listener's front room, thanks to the simple miracle of radio. As one lady in Norwich said of the two-week broadcast we staged for several years, live each evening from the Playhouse Bar during the Norfolk and Norwich Festival, 'I've never been to a Festival event – but I feel as if I have now.' She was pleased; we were tickled pink. We'd done all we set out to do!

Broadcasting from the Playhouse Bar during the Norfolk and Norwich Festival

Whether it's a big outside broadcast, a concert, a sell-out show at the Theatre Royal, a quiz programme, a church service with a congregation of 600, or one of the exhibitions staged by Gary Standley and the Action Desk team, Radio Norfolk and its colourful radio car and outside broadcast van have been there since day one.

In fact, it all began even before day one. Radio Norfolk went on air with test transmissions from the Royal Norfolk Show, three months before the official switch on in September 1980. Peter Glanville, one of the team who founded the station, was able to negotiate this experiment. Keith Skipper and Lesley Dolphin also did a 'dry run' from the new Queen Elizabeth Hospital in King's Lynn, just to test everything out in those pioneering days.

Show time: first ever stand at the Royal Norfolk Show

The Royal Norfolk showground has been a big feature over the years. For most of that time we've been there for the annual county show, where our stand, near the Dereham gate, became a place of pilgrimage. In 2001 the event was cancelled as a result of the foot and mouth outbreak, and the following year we had to pull out because the dates clashed with the big move of Radio Norfolk from Surrey Street to The Forum. It was a blessing in disguise, since the local radio van, which we'd used for many years, had rusted into radio history.

For 2004 and 2005, we teamed up with the Norfolk County Council marquee instead, while the 'radio buggy' gave presenters plenty of chances to broadcast from all over the showground. Mike Nichols rides shotgun on the buggy and makes sure the battery doesn't go flat at the wrong moment. Mike retired from the BBC once, but somehow has never really left and, frankly, we're not quite sure how we'd manage without him.

Show stopper: Wally Webb at the Royal Norfolk Show

Wally Webb and so many others recall the terrible year of 1985 when it rained non-stop, and the showground became a quagmire, like something from the Battle of the Somme. Presenters and county ladies in high-heeled shoes went slip-sliding away, and tractors had to be brought in to rescue vehicles from the car park. Keith Skipper remembers three of his contributors trapped at the stand because they couldn't slither out – it was that bad.

As Keith says, we always had a captive audience in those days – most of them queuing for the toilets opposite the Radio Norfolk stand – and Stand 38 was a good place to rest awhile at the end of the day, and watch Roy Waller's capers. Equally, people enjoyed Keith and his *Dinnertime* crew, who each year took part in a kind of repertory company play or music hall.

'It was the great coming together of presenters and listeners – all those people who wrote letters to us during the year. It was a case of putting letters to faces,' says Keith.

Keith Skipper preparing for Pantoland after escaping from cell 33

David Clayton remembers with a shudder one of the early years, 1984 to be precise, and an attempt to recreate the award-winning *Norfolk Airline* show at the show ground:

As the disc-jockey half of the presentation partnership, I felt we should replicate the idea of me sitting at the turntables and Neil [Walker] beside me – much as we did in the *Airline* studio. The engineers constructed an OB [outside broadcast] desk like a wrap-around disco console, and there I sat to start the *Airline*. It was 9 am, still a bit chilly despite being sunny. We did the introduction to the programme over the signature tune on a tape cartridge – fine, then I played in the first record. Thirty seconds into the tune, a gust of wind blew the record pick-up arm right across the surface of the disc with the usual scraping-across-a-record type sound. I was mortified. Neil Walker was unsure what was going on. We covered up as best we could and moved on, only to have someone phone in back at the studio and complain it was the most amateurish radio he'd ever heard. He was probably right!

The showground is also home in early September to the Old Car Rally, which is part of the annual Police Gala Day and the biggest event by far staged by the station. It all began in the very early days when the then young presenter David Clayton happened to wax lyrical about old cars. A phone-in led to a phenomenon. The Old Car Rally was born and since then has attracted record numbers of much loved motors with their gleaming chromium plating. Cars that were the latest models in the showroom back in those early days now qualify to take part, and do. David says:

After 25 of them, we've had precious few mishaps, considering the precarious nature of broadcasting in the middle of a field. I've always been amazed at how unfazed car owners are when approached by me wielding a microphone. The Jowett Javelin car has loomed large in my enthusiasm for old cars over the years, so I suppose when the chance came to drive one round a field while broadcasting, this was the pinnacle of my old car OB experience. However, coping with a column gearshift while holding a microphone was beyond me.

Veterans: Tony Mallion with a fine example of an entry for the Old Car Rally

We've been fortunate over the years to share the enthusiasm of Dinky Toy expert David Cooke on various programmes. He's been a regular at the car rally, dealing with the scaled-down versions of vehicles for 20 years:

> Some really fabulous collections have come in over the years, including some Foden vans, which were worth between £100 and £200, because they'd been so well looked after. We always get lots of television-linked vehicles and, appropriately, lots of farm machinery too. It's always a good day out and people like to put a face to the name.

On the technical side some broadcasts – like the car rally – can be quite simple, involving the radio car and a radio mike beaming in to one of our receivers. Others can be very complicated, involving miles of cabling and engineering man-hours. Take a Viennese-style concert with a full orchestra staged at Great Yarmouth's Britannia Pier, as part of a week of early summer events in the town. Station manager, Keith Salmon, thought this would be good event to record for broadcast on New Year's Day.

The Britannia Theatre is at the far end of the wooden pier and, for safety's sake, no vehicles are ever allowed on wooden seaside piers. This meant the outside broadcast van was parked on the promenade, with every bit of cable we could lay our hands on being linked up to reach not only to the theatre, but then up into the stage fly-tower and roof high above the orchestra. Three engineers were needed for this event, headed by John Adamson with David Brown and Colin ('Don't worry mate, it will be all right') Bolton. John discovered the main microphone, suspended from the theatre's ceiling, was the wrong way round. That involved another Spiderman-type crawl through the roof trusses.

The Lord Mayor's procession through the streets of Norwich in July is another annual fixture. Mercifully the rain doesn't usually fall on this parade. With two or three liveried Radio Norfolk vehicles and a public address system, it's a great way for presenters to say a loud 'hello' to the thousands who line the streets, while others go alongside with collecting buckets. There was a year when a Radio Norfolk bus was used, which proved a mistake, since no one could see the presenters stuck inside. On another occasion one of Jimmy Key's traction engines was borrowed from the Strumpshaw museum, giving a whole new meaning to the idea of 'steam radio'.

Keith Skipper liked to talk about broadcasting from Cell 33, as he dubbed Studio 1A at Norfolk Tower. A guest came in one day and said it was ' a bit like a prison cell' and Cell 33 it became. But then came the idea of taking the programme to Norwich Prison. It took a great deal of slicing through red tape, but finally we came to an agreement with the Home Office. Prison warders, prison visitors, the governor and inmates were all interviewed to capture the flavour of life inside.

Big occasions have warranted outside broadcasts. In 1989, ahead of the first European elections, I took the mid-morning *Countywide* programme to Strasbourg and the European Parliament building. Station manager, Keith Salmon, and programme assistant, Sue Boulton, completed the team. At that time Jimmy Young was always flying off to exotic locations. I decided we could follow his example by doing Monday's show and then boarding a plane at Norwich Airport shortly afterwards in order to be ready for the live broadcast on Wednesday. All would have been well, but for an engine failure at Holland's Schipol Airport, which meant a night in an Amsterdam hotel and considerable delay. The Norfolk euro MP, Paul Howell, met us off the plane the next day in a Mercedes limo and we soon caught up. It was amazing the freedom we had to wander round the inside of the building, bumping into characters like Dr Ian Paisley and simply knocking on the door of the late Barbara Castle (smoking her head off yet still looking glamorous) to make sure she was available to join us in the parliament's radio studio.

For the wedding of Charles and Diana, it was decided to broadcast the *Dinnertime* show live from the Crown public house in Norwich. Where else? But, as Keith Skipper recalls, with ale flowing freely in this mood of celebration, it was difficult to find people who could string three words together after two hours. Came the message in his headphones: 'Keep talking – the next guest isn't in a fit state.'

More recently, in 2004 *Today in Norfolk* headed to Normandy to mark the anniversary of D-Day. Graham Barnard was the presenter, with Lyn McKinney and Nicky Price sharing the production duties. Graham reflects:

The word OB – if it is actually a word – can mean different things to different people. To some, it's a chance to break the ties of the studio and actually get out and see some of the county we broadcast to, for others it's an opportunity to 'take on' temperamental broadcasting equipment and see if you can win! I knew that when we took the breakfast show to Normandy the

French connection: Graham and Nicky in Normandy

technical side of things would all run smoothly – and it did, but let's not get into the 'how come you can broadcast from Normandy without a hitch, when trying to broadcast from Chapelfield Gardens in Norwich can be fraught with difficulties' debate.

Instead, I know Lyn McKinney, Nicky Price and I will never forget any minute of that programme, and the preparation that went into it beforehand. Nicky and Lyn had pulled off one amazing production job, spending weeks setting it all up, much of it done in their own time. They'd become engrossed and moved by the stories of courage and loss. French-speaking Nicky arrived in France a day or two before Lyn and I caught the ferry. On the day before the actual programme, the three of us tore around the countryside to talk to Norfolk veterans, who had such moving stories to tell.

During the show itself, aside from the occasional realisation we were broadcasting to Norfolk from the other side of the Channel, we all felt humbled to be in the presence of these ordinary men who didn't think what they did for us was anything special. It was just something they had to do. But it took a great deal of effort to hold things together during those two-and-a-half hours on air, as the three of us stood so close to the beach where the Norfolk men had landed. It wasn't because of any impending technical crisis, but our own emotions that threatened to cause dead air. What an experience that OB was! It changed us all.

Lyn Mckinney stayed on:

Having waved goodbye to Graham and Nicky in the market place in Arromanches, I moved inland to the hotel in Caen where the 1st Norfolks were staying over the D-Day anniversary weekend ... and, using the Radio Norfolk estate car, which attracted greetings wherever I went, I reported into news and weekend programmes, accompanying the veterans as they visited cemeteries and old military encampments.

On the morning of the 60th anniversary of D-Day itself, we gathered near Bellevue Farm for the unveiling of a memorial to over a hundred men who'd died there. Not a cloud in the sky – just a gentle breeze rippling the poppies in the cornfield behind, reminding us of the sacrifice those men had made. It was very humbling ... and everywhere the Norfolks went, they were greeted by the French people as heroes. One woman said, 'They are old, yes, but for us, they will always be young', and the granddaughter of a French farmer who hosts a lunch every year for returning veterans told me, 'Without them, quite simply we would not be here.'

Norfolk Regiment memorial

For many years New Year's Eve was marked with a broadcast from the party at the Great Yarmouth Marina Centre, with Wally Webb, David Clayton, Roy Waller and Olly Day among the turntables and balloons. But with the Millennium, all that changed and I was charged with providing through-the-night broadcasting to mark this momentous event.

The Cassandras were warning us that the whole world could grind to a halt at midnight; computers could stop and civil unrest could break out. We had to prepare for that 'just-in-case' moment, while the jollity continued. Roy Waller was on the steps of City Hall for the big countdown; Graham Barnard was out at street parties in Norwich; Jim Cassidy was trying to see if there was any life at all in Great Yarmouth – there was, once the fireworks went off and the town suddenly woke up – while I was in the studio linking it all together with the Bishop of Thetford, the Rt Rev. Hugo de Vaal.

There were many moments to treasure, including the family who were alone on Blakeney Point to see the year 2000 arrive, who joined us by phone. We also spoke to Norfolk's organiser-in-chief, Bruno Peek, who was on the Thames

Tony Mallion at the Millennium Dome

masterminding beacons and looking after the Queen. Once Her Majesty arrived at Greenwich, Bruno was on the phone to us. We'd seen him with the Queen on our television sets in the studio. From Bruno came the classic line, 'It was just like chatting to my mum.'

The Queen was heading for the ill-fated Millennium Dome. I'd broadcast from there in September as the construction continued. Assistant Kate Prout ensured it all went remarkably smoothly, yet it was obvious, even before it opened, that the enterprise was a huge white elephant. It still made for a great OB.

Radio Norfolk holidays were popular big events for many years, and often produced live broadcasts or recorded programmes. Weekends at Potters Leisure Resort in Hopton, with presenters and their families enjoying mixing with the listeners, were always a big hit. There were round-the-world trips; railway holidays in Scotland; trips to the United States and Holland, and the biggest of them all – four coaches and 160 listeners on a once-in-a-lifetime visit to the Holy Land, with both the Bishop of Norwich and the Roman Catholic Bishop of East Anglia accompanying the tour. The physical as well as the spiritual was catered for, with a doctor also on board.

Tony Mallion with listeners on the Holy Land tour

Who could ever forget the Garden Tomb and the place where they laid Jesus? Or floating on – rather than swimming in – the mineral-rich Dead Sea? I was trying to make a recording while floating on my back but, with arms aloft, I felt myself slipping sideways, with the danger that the cassette machine could end up under some extremely salty water. The Bishop of Norwich, Peter Nott, came to my rescue and righted me, like some lifeboat. I always thought it was rather appropriate to be saved by a bishop in the Holy Land.

Equally memorable was a visit in 1990 to Oberammergau for the Passion Play. Lyn McKinney was one of the guides:

> The Passion Play has been performed every 10 years since 1634, in thanksgiving for delivery from the Black Death. I was the fourth member of the BBC team accompanying the trip, the others being manager, Keith Salmon and his wife Denise, and the Rev. Grahame Humphries, our religious producer. We flew into Salzburg Airport and spent a few days at St Georgen, near Lake Attersee.
>
> In the Salzkammergut region of Upper Austria, made famous by the film *The Sound of Music*, our guide Jan, very patiently and with great good humour, organised day trips to Vienna and Salzburg for us, as well as showing us around the very beautiful lakes and mountains. I discovered a passion for freshwater trout cooked in garlic, and the knee-slapping evening at the hotel was a riot!
>
> The village of Oberammergau in Upper Bavaria is unique, with many of the buildings painted with frescoes of Biblical scenes – so many demands on your camera! Five thousand people watch every performance of Christ's passion, acted on a stage that is open to the elements, and it takes all day. We, the audience, were provided with a translation from the German, and were seated under cover – the thousand-strong cast was made up of the people from the village, and many of the men grow their hair for months in the hopes of being picked to play Jesus. There's a choir and an orchestra that plays music

composed by a local teacher nearly 200 years ago. I have never seen anything like it before or since. It truly was a moving and amazing performance, of a very high standard, and I was glad I'd had the opportunity to see it performed in my lifetime.

Church services are great excuses to get out and about. Congregations usually enjoy the extra excitement of a live broadcast or recording. For Easter 2003, we went to the large Cromer Parish Church, with a congregation of over 300 people. A last-minute hitch with a computer back at base meant they thought it was live when it wasn't – but, by a miracle, our engineer, Paul Whitworth, had remembered to bring a recorder in the van. At the end I had to stand up and tell them all the bad news, 'You weren't going out live', and the good news, 'You can hear yourselves – we'll put out the recording at three this afternoon.' That's one way to increase listenership.

There was one church – which shall remain nameless – where the vicar had upset the organist before the service. The upshot was a live service with a small congregation who didn't really want to sing. I had to urge them. We just about got through it. At Acle Parish Church we recorded a special service for Christmas Day. Twice in the van a strange voice appeared on the speakers over the singing. Having decided it wasn't a message from the Almighty, sound engineer, Bob Castleton, suggested we might be picking up a rogue radio-mike. I dashed off to the church hall where, sure enough, there was conjuror entertaining a children's party. He was a bit surprised to see me, especially when I had to join in his act to explain that we were picking up his microphone. He switched it off – bless him!

We've regularly broadcast or recorded at Norwich Cathedral for big events, including the ordination of women priests, which involved almost a week's worth of cable-laying by engineers, Lionel Scott and Mike Nichols. Jill Bennett and the Rev. Grahame Humphries were our very able commentators from their lofty perch high up in the building. We were also there for the Maundy Thursday service attended by the Queen.

More recently the 9/11 service, the death of the Queen Mother and the memorial service for the Asian tsunami victims meant hastily scrambling our cathedral team of Stewart Orr and Mike Nichols, with the bishop's chaplain, the Rev. Jan McFarlane, as a very smooth commentator. We were there for the centenary service for Norwich City, when the choir sang 'On the Ball City' like never before – the congregation failed to manage the usual lusty version heard from the Barclay end – and Stewart thoughtfully provided green and yellow gaffer tape to secure the cables to the floor. We got an award for that service.

The Bygone Village at Fleggburgh – sadly an attraction no more – offered us its 500-seat Regent Theatre, complete with a mighty Compton cinema organ. It was a perfect location for a couple of highly atmospheric Christmas services involving Canon Ivan Bailey, the Rev. Rosemary Wakelin, other local clergy and the Broadland Youth Choir under the direction of founder Carol Timms. But the building also housed a full-size Savage's traditional roundabout. Now where else could you sing carols and then take a trip on a merry-go-round in the interval? It was hard to get the children's choir and the audience back! We also used this venue for our 20th-birthday celebrations with a variety show and – the next morning – a service.

The Bygone Village was also the first place that we teamed up with the Band of the Dragoon Guards after they'd made Norfolk their home. The concert marked our 21st birthday, but that proved a day to remember for a terrible reason – it was *the* 11 September. We went ahead with the concert after a minute's silence. David Clayton was there, having only just returned from taking his son James for a weekend to New York, and a trip to the top of the Twin Towers – clearly one of the last to ever do so.

That association with the Dragoons continued right up to their final concert in August, which we staged at Norwich Cathedral. It was an honour when

Olly Day with Postman Pat and collectors for the charity Children in Need

Wally, Nicky and Kirstee involved with the 2004 Children in Need campaign

the Dragoons asked us to organise this last concert for them. We little realised it would sell out over two months beforehand.

The Dragoons took part in a big *Children in Need* show at the Theatre Royal and provided a colourful finale. Since then we've staged gala shows there for our annual Toys and Tins appeal with the Salvation Army. Major Ray Begley, the leader of the Army in Norwich, is a former West End dancer and choreographer, so ideal to work alongside. But we do get a bit carried away with the size of cast. Backstage at the Theatre Royal must be something like Dr Who's Tardis, when it successfully absorbs a cast of 300!

Gary Standley and his Action Desk team have seized the opportunities The Forum provides with successful history fairs, a wartime celebration and gardening events that have seen entire tropical gardens recreated indoors. And he's twice used the outdoor vegetation of Chapelfield Gardens as a backdrop for BBC *Wild in Your Garden* events.

I love theatres and because of that I am proud of the fact that, in the days before Radio Suffolk, when we covered the Waveney Valley, we had the first broadcast from the newly restored Marina Theatre at Lowestoft. In my days as a reporter on the *Lowestoft Journal*, I'd championed the idea of the old ABC cinema becoming a civic theatre to replace the ageing (and freezing) Sparrow's Nest. It was something the Lowestoft Players championed and, some 15 years later, it happened. One of the local councillors, Andree Maillard Back, was a keen supporter of the idea as well as being a professional singer. It was she who gave the very first performance from that stage live, for Radio Norfolk, on the day before the official opening of the theatre. A few years later I was able to broadcast from the King's Lynn Corn Exchange – Norfolk's finest concert hall – ahead of its opening.

Theatres are usually the venue for our daft panel game *Should the Team Think?* which was dreamt up by Keith Skipper and David Clayton over a pint or three some 14 years ago and first unleashed on an unsuspecting public at Hunstanton's Princess Theatre. It's a bit like every other panel game you've ever heard with its own Norfolk twist like 'Just a Minute and a Half' and 'Call Me an old Bluffer', with the team trying to define ancient Norfolk words.

It's always relied on the quick wit of Sid Kipper, with Keith Skipper, Roy Waller and David Clayton having been other constant fixtures – apart from the occasion when David fell down some stairs and I had to stand in at short notice. Patrick Anthony, Canon Ivan Bailey, Olly Day and Peter Glanville have also taken part. Stephen Bumfrey has now become a regular. The show's toured round the area since then, visiting Gorleston Pavilion, Watton Queen's Hall, Sheringham Little Theatre, Saxlingham Nethergate Village Hall and Norwich's Playhouse and Maddermarket Theatre. It's never failed to have the audiences roaring with laughter.

Now we know that it's going to be all right, both on the night and also when I've finished editing it down for broadcast. But as David Clayton recalls, he wasn't that confident on the first occasion:

> I remember standing in the wings of the Princess Theatre with an auditorium full of our listeners expecting an hilarious night. I was the chairman so had to go on first. Keith Skipper and I had planned *Should the Team Think?* but in all honesty had no idea if it would really work. People had paid good money to see us and to say there were butterflies in my stomach was an understatement. I remember wondering why we were putting ourselves through this torture. I was introduced and walked on to a thunderous round of applause. I cracked a feeble gag and a loud guffaw came back from the attentive audience – we were off and running. Although it's a recording, it has all the tensions of an OB and after all these years its the best fun five ageing blokes can have with their clothes on!

It was fun doing an OB from Blackpool Pleasure Beach, a meticulously planned broadcast by assistant, Nancy Stolworthy, who sent John Cushing and myself up the famous Tower, onto the trams and the Pepsi Max 'Big One' roller-coaster at the Pleasure Beach. Nancy did all this without leaving her desk in Norwich, with the aid of a Blackpool street map and a telephone. I had to pre-record the nerve-wracking trip on the roller-coaster, using a lip mike and cassette recorder, seated alongside press officer Helen O'Neil and hoping I wouldn't knock my teeth out in the process. I'd been warned it couldn't be done and I was determined to prove them wrong. As I staggered off, John Cushing told me I hadn't recorded a thing and would have to do it all again.

Great Yarmouth's Hippodrome Circus – my favourite place – has featured in many a broadcast, but on one occasion I suggested I sat on a trapeze that would be lowered to the ring floor. I little realised that engineer Lionel Scott and Hippodrome owner Peter Jay were plotting behind my back. I sat down and was strapped on for safety's sake, even though it was to be – as I thought – only a foot or two off the ground. Peter pressed a button and the trapeze was hoisted aloft some 50 feet (15 m) above the ring! My gasp was the real thing, as my stomach disappeared through the balls of my feet and I proved I was neither the daring nor young man on the flying trapeze.

Over the years, between us we've staged countless outside broadcasts and big events that we hope have captured the atmosphere for the listeners. Often it means reaching the parts that you – or we – would never reach. And that was so true of my favourite OB, an idea suggested by Jill Bennett and put into practice by Alison Walker and Lyn McKinney, with engineering from David Brown. We went to Felbrigg Hall, near Cromer, to celebrate the start of the National Trust's centenary year – and we went in December when it was closed to the public. What a privilege it was to have the house, with its protective dust jackets, to ourselves, and to venture into the cellars and the attics. I could have stayed there forever and I'll never forget describing the scene to *Today in Norfolk* and Jim Cassidy, with the sun rising through the early mist over the Norfolk countryside as only it can on a still December morning.

It's moments like that which are special for us; make all the hard work and planning worthwhile and, above all, create something special for you as well. Now, where is that soldering iron?

Where are they now?
Keith Salmon

Ten years ago, the first working day of retirement seemed very odd. A warm glow still lingered from the more-than-generous farewell party, but this was now Monday morning. The 34-year connection with the BBC had ended and for the first time there was no job to go to. It did seem odd.

But there was a cunning plan. First, keep busy: the builders arrived to replace the roof at home and I became the self-styled site manager. Secondly, don't look back: there was a life outside the Beeb. And for me this life would involve a return to academic study (having vowed never to sit another exam after my first degree all those years ago).

The following autumn I enrolled with UEA's extra-mural studies department to seek a diploma in Art History. For the next two years I motored across to Fakenham each Monday evening to a most enjoyable class, though I never quite came to terms with the modern fashion for students to give the lectures; it was never thus in the fifties.

Taking note: Keith Salmon

With diploma in hand, I then bit the bullet, gave up this leisurely approach to learning and set about reading for a full-scale Master of Arts degree at UEA. It began with another diploma – a one-year full-time graduate course – and then two years of part-time study for the MA. It was a very happy and fruitful time, and I became completely besotted with the twelfth century, its art and literature.

Since then life has become more involved with family: trips to see our younger daughter and her family at her home among the ski resorts of Colorado; trips to our sister-in-law now living permanently in France and more recently, trips to London to our other daughter to help in bringing up our grandson. And when time permits we chug around the Broads in our elderly motor cruiser. One day I may take to gardening, but don't hold your breath.

Where are they now?
Lesley Dolphin

I joined BBC Radio Norfolk at the very start – I had been waiting for them to advertise for staff ever since coming home from Yorkshire in 1979. While at college in Bradford, I had got my first taste of working for local radio and was determined to be there when the BBC got under way in my home county.

Luckily for me, the first editor of the station, Mike Chaney, gave me a job – as station assistant. This was great training, because it involved all sorts of work, from reporting live with the radio car to 'twiddling the knobs' for a live programme. I've so many memories, some of them lighthearted, like recording a donkey that used to come into a pub for a drink and John Mountford presenting the breakfast show from a waterbed. Others were more tragic, like the helicopter crash off the coast that killed 12 people.

I was at Radio Norfolk for four years and during my last couple of years was asked to present the *Afternoon Show*. I loved working for BBC local radio from the very start, but to work as a presenter was absolutely fantastic. We took the show on the road across Norfolk, and I met some great guests, including celebrities visiting the county. Morecambe and Wise took the mickey for ten minutes without me drawing breath; Diana Dors and Billy Connolly are just some of the other names I remember. However during my four years with Radio Norfolk I also got married and then became pregnant with my first son – hence my departure in 1984.

Present day Lesley

I haven't moved far since then – just across the border to Suffolk. I now live in Ipswich – and yes I do support the Blues these days rather than City – sorry, Mr Waller. I am married to Mark Murphy, who presents the breakfast show for BBC Radio Suffolk, and I present the mid-morning show between 10.00 and 1.00 pm. I still really enjoy my work for BBC local radio, and when I visit Lowestoft, I still meet people who remember my days working for Radio Norfolk – over 20 years ago!

Chapter 8
A question of sport
Matthew Gudgin

My awareness of Radio Norfolk sports coverage began with the very first weekend of the station's existence. The excitement surrounding a new local radio service made all the programmes a must listen, but Norwich City's home match that first Saturday was Radio Norfolk's debut outside broadcast. I remember hearing some catchy up-beat music played to introduce the programme. Rob Bonnet was the host of *Saturday Special* and Roy Waller, with Keith Skipper, commentated live from Carrow Road. Norwich were playing Southampton and won 1–0, and the winning goal was scored by Justin Fashanu. The style and immediacy of the sports show struck a chord straight away. The sheer novelty of having a whole programme devoted to your local team was terrific. I was only 11 years old at the time, but followed the Canaries avidly through the Radio Norfolk programmes.

The first big Norwich success for Radio Norfolk to cover was in 1985 – victory at Wembley in the Milk Cup final. Unusually, the big match was being televised but, like many fans, I switched off the television sound and listened to Roy's commentary. One of the highlights was John Bond's unforgettable exclamation when City were one nil up with just minutes to go. As Roy took a pause for breath, the Canary manager burst in with, 'Come on ref, blow your bloody whistle!'

The referee eventually obliged, and Mike Souter grabbed his microphone, rushed out onto the hallowed Wembley turf and exhorted the legendary Mick Channon to give him a big hug.

The Radio Norfolk Saturday afternoon sports programme was a firm fixture when I joined the team in 1987. Allowed to assist in the backroom, making coffee and collating scores, I was thrilled to be working with presenters Malcolm Robertson and Mike Ward. Malcolm was a sports journalist *par excellence*, with a great passion for the Canaries. His professionalism and attention to detail were a fine lesson to anyone starting out.

Mike was a great character who chain-smoked in the office and always had a plastic cup of coffee on the go. He was an unflappable broadcaster and could talk knowledgeably about any sport, especially rugby. Mike didn't stand on ceremony. I recall him stubbing his cigarette out on a grass-court at a posh tennis club, ignoring the disapproving looks of the members. At another event he discarded his lighted fag, and set fire to some undergrowth next to the pitch! The St John's Ambulance crew were left to beat out the flames with their blankets.

Mike Ward's other Radio Norfolk incarnation was as quiz master. His *Sporting Chance* series pitted teams from around the county against each other in a local version of *Question of Sport.* Mike was always introduced as 'your genial host'. He always made sure the venues for *Sporting Chance* had a well stocked bar!

Malcolm Robertson's commentary highlight came at Highbury in 1989 when the Norwich City players became embroiled in a furious punch-up with their Arsenal opponents.

'It's mayhem, absolute mayhem out there,' Malcolm's passionate description of the fracas continued, with fellow commentator Richard Henwood trying unsuccessfully to be heard above the din.

Saturday Special: Roy Waller and Rob Bonnet at Carrow Road

My chief role in those years was a technical one, operating the equipment at our homely Norfolk Tower studios. I well remember being in the studio for the 1989 FA Cup semi-final against Everton, which was completely overshadowed by the Hillsborough disaster that same day. Everyone was stunned by the news coming from the other match, and silence descended on the Radio Norfolk newsroom.

John Taylor: bowls legend

Eventually the BBC allowed me on air, and the first programme I presented was *Friday Sport*, which included one of the great enduring features of our sports output, the bowls report with John Taylor. John's love of bowls is legendary on Radio Norfolk – he's covered Middleton Cup matches all round the country. Being a traditionalist, who looked askance when coloured clothing was introduced for the Norfolk team, he made some pithy comments when the Hopton venue for the World Championship was officially opened with loud music and a knockabout comedy routine! On that first programme, I also recall Jean Harris with tennis, Reg Snowling and his snooker feature, and athletics with Brendan Byrne.

Being sent to Norwich's Trowse training ground was a daunting prospect, but the then City manager, Dave Stringer, put me at my ease and provided a friendly introduction to covering the Canaries. Trowse was very basic, and a far cry from City's modern Colney training centre. The door to the dressing-rooms closed with an almighty bang and ruined many an interview. If it wasn't the Trowse door, then the sugar beet lorries on the Lowestoft road, which ran past the ground, provided even more of a din.

Meeting and interviewing some of the legends of world sport has been a great honour. Many of the big names have made their way to the county over the years. I was dispatched to the Hewett School one wet and windy Tuesday afternoon to cover a youth football training event, only to discover that Sir Bobby Charlton was taking the session. Sir Bobby wore his fame lightly. He asked where he should stand for the interview and proceeded to talk as if he was just any other footballer. Another World Cup winner, Sir Geoff Hurst, came to St Andrew's High School at Thorpe many years later. The children swarmed all over him for autographs, even though most of their parents weren't even alive when he scored that famous hat-trick at Wembley. Sir Geoff had fond memories of playing against Norwich in the sixties and seventies, and particularly of the hard time he got from City's tough-tackling centre-half Duncan Forbes!

It was a dream come true when I was told to cover the Norfolk county cricket team in 1988. All the home matches were staged at the historic Lakenham ground in Norwich. The crowd were friendly, the weather usually perfect and the surroundings were picturesque. I reported back to the studio via a mobile telephone, which was the size of a hi-fi speaker. The battery was forever running flat and more than once I had to sprint down the road to the nearest telephone-box. The only problem with reporting on Norfolk cricket in those days was the success rate of the team. The County were going through a lean period, and I didn't see them win for a couple of years.

Again, I was lucky with interviewees: Stephen Plumb was a cheerful and pleasant Norfolk captain, as well as being an outstanding all-rounder; and Brian Lara was an important visiting player at Lakenham. The world-record-breaking batsman spoke to us when he was in the Warwickshire side playing the Minor Counties. Midway through our conversation, my mobile phone started ringing. I was mortified and fumbled in my pocket to switch it off. Lara didn't seem to bother – he shrugged his shoulders in a typical Caribbean manner and continued with the interview.

Sadly Lakenham was forced to close its doors to cricket in 2000, after more than 150 years. Radio Norfolk marked the occasion with its first ever ball-by-ball broadcast. The star of *Test Match Special*, Henry Blofeld, was drafted in to lead the commentary. A rickety scaffold tower was built at the pavilion end for us to view the game. 'Blowers' was in top form, likening one of our Norfolk players to a Chieftain tank and waxing lyrical about the pigeons. Then, as the last delivery was about to be bowled at Lakenham, a large propeller-driven aircraft flew low over the ground, prompting more poetic descriptions from Henry.

Henry joined us again at Lords for Norfolk's victory over Devon in the 2001 Minor Counties Knockout final and once more for a C and G Trophy match against Kent at Manor Park. That latter commentary was nearly scuppered from the start when, in full flow at the start of the game, Henry's view was completely obscured by the re-positioning of the sightscreen in front of our commentary box! It really was an enormous privilege for all of us to work with the legendary 'Blowers'.

Howzat! Chris, Matthew and Nicky at Lords

Radio Norfolk broadcast live coverage from both of Norfolk's cup-final wins at Lords. The first in 1997 saw Nick Bowler and myself enjoy the wonderful experience of reporting from John Arlott's box in the ornate Victorian splendour of the Lords Pavilion. We nearly didn't make it for the second day of the match, after making the mistake of joining the Norfolk team in the hotel bar for most of the night. They sprinted out onto the field like spring lambs the next morning. Nick and I were not so sprightly, as we struggled up the pavilion steps to the box!

Roy Waller's contribution to the Radio Norfolk success story over 20 years is mentioned many times in this book. In the field of football commentary, few could match his dedication and longevity. A Norwich supporter through and through, Roy's highlight must be the UEFA Cup run of 1993. Trips to the Olympic Stadium in Munich and the San Siro in Milan took Roy to some of the European temples of sport. First Division duties have taken him to some less glamorous parts of the globe. Commentating from a shed on top of the stand at Port Vale, climbing up a 30-foot (9 m) ladder to get to the gantry at Swansea, and attempting to describe 90 minutes through a Merseyside pea-souper at Tranmere would have tested lesser men to their limits.

Over the last dozen seasons or so, Roy has followed the Canaries at home and away, clocking up many thousands of miles. After the bitter disappointment of Norwich's relegation from the Premiership in 1995, there followed a procession of nondescript seasons. The gloom was lifted with the arrival of Nigel Worthington, and Roy's untiring obsession with his beloved Norwich City eventually paid off, first with a never-to-be-forgotten trip to the play-off final against Birmingham in 2002 at the Millennium Stadium in Cardiff, where Norwich was defeated in a heartbreaking penalty shootout, and then a couple of years later when Norwich won the Division One title, which lifted them

Assessing the ref, Roy Waller at Carrow Road

back to their rightful place in the top-flight. Unfortunately for one season only – let us hope they will soon be back.

Chris Goreham had the difficult task of interviewing the crestfallen players out on the pitch immediately after the shootout at Cardiff in 2002. It was a testimony to their professionalism that they all spoke to us after such a devastating experience.

BBC Radio Norfolk with the Canaries on the 2004 celebration bus

The *Scrimmage* programme, named from the lyrics of Norwich City's club anthem *On the Ball City*, has earned a big following on Thursday evenings. Chris has injected humour into the deadly serious world of football, with fans telling him about the Norwich City 'shrines' they have at home, and he revels in some of the nonsensical quotes uttered by some of our best known footballers.

Motor sport at Snetterton Circuit has often provided exciting material for our programmes. We covered the Willhire 25-Hour Race in 1989 – a mammoth event, with fans camping in tents overnight. *Saturday Special* was broadcast live from the track's 50th anniversary meeting in 2002. We chatted to one of Snetterton's great founding fathers, ex-Formula Three champion Jim Russell, who was a great educator in motor sport. He told us he'd masterminded all the special effects in James Garner's 1968 feature film, *Grand-Prix*. Jim worked out many of the stunts, and built the cars in Norfolk.

Our motor-racing reporter, David Bennett, has brought many events at Snetterton alive with his enthusiastic descriptions. Over the years we have heard from the son of an ex-world champion, Nelson Piquet Jr, the Bollywood film star who took time off to race cars in Britain. We have also taken you round the track in every conceivable vehicle, from a Jaguar two-seater to a racing Citroen 2-CV.

Edwin Overland is our voice of speedway. He follows the fortunes of the King's Lynn Stars in a colourful sport that is never far from controversy or incident. I love visiting the Saddlebow Road track for the noise and smell of the speedway. The bravery of the riders must never be underestimated in a dangerous sport that does not allow them the luxury of brakes! King's Lynn's promoter Buster Chapman is a great character and has joined us many times for lively phone-ins with the Stars' faithful.

Radio Norfolk has forged close relationships with many individual sportsmen and – women from the county who have gained national success. King's Lynn's own Martin Brundle enjoyed a decade on the Formula One grid, and appeared on our programme many times. Cassie Jackman from North Walsham was the queen of squash, winning 20 women's tour titles, as well as her crowning achievement in 1999, when she became world champion.

We have followed Barry Pinches' snooker career from his early days as amateur to the wonderful form he has shown in recent times, which has taken him to the verge of a place in the world's top 16. Barry's victory over Jimmy White at the Crucible in 2004 got him noticed, as did his trademark yellow and green waistcoat.

Norfolk has not produced many golfers, but Dereham's Andrew Marshall has established himself on the European tour and he has been happy to allow Radio Norfolk to share the ups and downs of life as an aspiring top player.

There was also Taverham tennis player, Chris Bailey, who took Goran Ivanisevic to match-point at Wimbledon. Chris is now a successful tennis commentator with BBC and Sky Sports.

Jon Thaxton gave us the excuse to mount our first-ever live boxing commentary in 2005. The lad from Sprowston achieved his dream of lifting the WBF World Lightweight title in front of a jubilant crowd at the Norwich Sports Village. Radio 5 boxing correspondent John Rawling was our guest commentator, bringing the moment alive with a memorable description when 'Jono' beat his French opponent. Unfortunately our post-fight analysis was cut short when the fire alarm went off, and everyone had to evacuate to the car park, bewildered but happy.

David Mann is a mushroom farmer from Bungay during

the week, but at the weekend he drives rally cars. Radio Norfolk has followed David's career for nearly 20 years and we were all delighted when he achieved his dream of winning the British Championship.

Semi-professional football has given us some great moments over three decades. There is a tremendous level of support and participation in dozens of local clubs across the county. Bill Ribbons was our local football correspondent in the early days, but since 1988 it has been Nick Bowler, who must have travelled to almost every ground in Norfolk.

The 1994 FA Vase final at Wembley was the biggest semi-professional game we have ever covered. Diss Town, nicknamed the 'Tangerines', won a dramatic final in extra time. Nick and Roy commentated from the Wembley gantry, relegating Norwich City's home match that afternoon to just a supporting role. The Diss manager, Bill Punton, proved a 'gift' to radio, always willing to speak and eloquent with it. A few years later we launched our *Local Report* programme on Friday evenings, with Bill as the co-presenter with Nick Bowler.

Nick Bowler: grass roots

Our commitment to King's Lynn FC has grown over the years. We now aim to broadcast at least half-a-dozen of the Linnets' matches in a season. Radio Norfolk was there when King's Lynn reached the FA Cup second round at Rotherham in 1998, when they won the Doc Martens Eastern Division title at Fisher Athletic in 2004, and the night they lifted the Southern League cup against Bedford Town in 2005. It is a well supported and well run club, and deserves to continue its progress up through the leagues.

So much has happened in Norfolk sport over 25 years that it's impossible to mention all the stories of success and failure, hope and despair that we've witnessed since 1980. But I am sure sport will continue to be an important ingredient in the Radio Norfolk success story for as long as people still support their local teams.

Where are they now?
Mike Sewell

If there was an end deeper than the deep end, then I was thrown into it on 14 February 1993. I was midway through college when I came into Norfolk Tower to talk to the then sports editor, Roger Ryan, to ask about the possibility of a short placement. He obliged, but as my ultimate aim was to be a football reporter and commentator, he urged me to come in the following Saturday to watch the sports programme go out on air.

You can imagine my shock, horror and fear when, upon arrival that Saturday lunchtime, he thrust a breezeblock of a mobile phone into my hand and said, 'I'm sending you to cover Fakenham v Brightlingsea.'

'You must be joking!' I thought to myself. But despite spending what was a freezing afternoon trying to find a place in the ground where no one could see or hear me, I got through and it was the start of my career.

I was a freelance for the whole of my three-and-a-half years, so took what I could to earn the money. As well as being the early bulletin sports reporter, I was briefly (thankfully) a news reporter, which provided me with possibly the worst day of my career. I was assigned the NHS figures for Norfolk. Say no more!

I presented *Saturday Sport, Saturday Stretch*, acted as sports editor, commentated on Norwich City, and even drove former presenter, Keith Skipper, to King's Lynn once a week to do his programme.

All I can say is that it was the best grounding I could have wished for and all the memories I have – apart from the NHS figures – are fond ones.

Where are they now?
Rob Bonnet

Hmm ... 25 years eh? Which silver anniversary are we talking about? My marriage to the BBC, to my wife Margie, or to the building society?

Six weeks before Radio Norfolk's grand opening, I'd been fretting about remembering my wedding vows at the altar. Theatrically, perhaps, we had decided to say them from memory, rather than repeat them after the priest. Wedding pictures show me white as a sheet, as I nervously slipped on the ring, stage fright I have never quite repeated since.

The day before, we had taken on our first mortgage on a terraced house off Norwich's Aylsham Road – £11,500 if I remember rightly. I wish it was the same figure now!

August went by in a flash and then, as Radio Norfolk came to its first transmission date, the heaviest responsibility of them all – the *Lunchtime Show*. Keith Skipper later called it the *Dinnertime* programme, for lunch was for metropolitan careerists.

I wrote in the *Radio Times* that we would not necessarily know what was going to be on the programme as we went into the studio at midday. On reflection, it was an insincere attempt to give the impression of a free-wheeling, fast-moving, pro-active, re-active, over-active, think-on-your-feet, fly-by-the-seat-of-your-pants programme. In reality, I preferred a running-order set in stone with jolly music and reliable guests, many of them ferried down from Norwich's Theatre Royal.

Potentially, French mime artist Marcel Marceau was challenging radio – strong on visuals but with an act conducted in absolute silence. First question? 'So, Marcel. Perhaps you could just demonstrate a few extracts from your show?' Tempting as it was to embark on a commentary ('and Marcel raises his hands flat against an imaginary pane of glass'), we talked instead and he was a charming and interesting guest. But the lesson was learned: mime – and probably also cooking – does not work especially well on the radio.

Body language: Rob Bonnet interviewing the mime artist Marcel Marceau

A few weeks later came the biggest match Carrow Road has ever staged – Radio Norfolk versus the Radio 1 All-Stars. The Ledwidge–Bonnet partnership (more Laurel and Hardy than Bertschin and Deehan) was well supplied by manager John Bond, and scored prolifically for a 5–2 win. Ten thousand fans were there and cheered to the crumbling rafters of the Main Stand but, curiously, the autograph hunters afterwards were only interested in John Peel, Peter Powell and Mike Read.

But the roar of the crowd and the smell of the liniment had been seductive. From that moment on, despite exciting moments door-stepping Margaret Thatcher and a flight in an airship to Great Yarmouth and back, I wanted to be a sports broadcaster, and so developed pointy elbows whenever access to the Carrow Road press box was available.

Norwich City, sadly, felt like the only story in town. Sure, there was minor counties cricket at Lakenham, speedway in King's Lynn and racing at Great Yarmouth, but the bluster of Canaries' chairman Sir Arthur South and the warmth of manager Ken Brown eventually became familiar.

Football coverage had been feeling its way. One test transmission, a couple of weeks before we went on air, experimented with a freelance reporter for Norwich's League Cup visit to Shrewsbury, where radio broadcasting was still an undiscovered art. From our man's first five seconds, I was praying that nobody was listening – which they probably weren't. In a painfully measured voice he monotoned, 'In the fifth minute, Norwich went close with an effort from Justin Fashanu. That's Fashanu … F-A-S-H-A-N-U. Point. Par.' Even the *EDP* copytaker would have struggled to stay awake.

Once transmissions were for real, the coverage became more energised. The legendary Roy Waller was still an AA man at the time, and just occasionally he'd revert to the vocabulary of his day-job with phrases like 'another breakdown in the Norwich defence' or 'there goes McGuire motoring through midfield'. But quickly Rodeo Roy realised there was more to life than saluting from the roadside, and he joined the Radio Norfolk team – a job that allowed him the occasional free afternoon on the tennis courts of Waterloo Park, where I'd give him a good thrashing. 'Ooh, I say,' he'd exclaim as another forehand fizzed past his left ear. The style was more Frankie Howerd than Dan Maskell, but this was commentary talent in the making nevertheless.

Sometimes – of course – I made a complete jimmy of myself. One afternoon soon after we went on air, I was in the studio with Kevin Bond, the manager's son, and a centre-half of sound professional ability, but – it has to be said – of limited finesse. The previous day I'd picked up a bit of tittle-tattle at the training ground, when I heard someone call him 'Dobbin' – affectionately, I thought. So, in a moment of naïve curiosity, I asked him about the nickname. He shot me a look that said something like, 'Are you trying to take the **** or what?' I let it pass, but years later, when crowds were braying at Arsenal's Tony Adams, the penny finally dropped – at which point I realised that a broadcaster can be a donkey too!

Meanwhile, we were developing ambitions a little beyond our technical abilities. Late in the 1980–81 season Norwich had an Easter Monday home match with Ipswich, and the programme, I insisted, had to be presented, music and all, from the Carrow Road television gantry. And so the record turntables were hauled into the roof of the South Stand and the microphones linked to the stadium PA.

All of which was fine until the start of the match, but once Carrow Road was rocking to its foundations in the excitement of a 1–0 home win, the record stylus and its arm took on lives of their own. What's more, my four-letter frustration briefly found itself broadcast on the stadium loudspeakers. Now

Radio Norfolk has its own five-star studio, where the only dilemma is what to choose from Delia's lunch menu.

I left Radio Norfolk in the spring of 1982 for a brief spell on Radio 1's *Newsbeat*, and every morning meeting dealt with news from the Falklands, which was certainly a whole world away from the latest intrigue on Breckland District Council. By the autumn, I found myself working with my heroes on BBC Radio Sport, J. Peter Jones and Bryon Butler, neither of whom – sadly – are still with us. Briefly, I yearned for a career as a football commentator alongside them. Wisely, my London bosses resisted any temptation to risk me on Radio 2, but at the end of Norwich's Milk Cup season of 1985, an opportunity arose.

Rodeo Roy must have been unavailable for Chelsea v. Norwich at Stamford Bridge, the very last game of the season and a meaningless match for both teams. So I took my place for Radio Norfolk, high in a practically deserted East Stand with Mick Channon, and doubtless delivered every commentary cliché under the sun several times over. I had to look up the result just now to remember it: 2–1 to Norwich, in fact. Far more memorable was the fact that the game would surely have been abandoned had it not been so inconsequential, for a downpour had turned the pitch into a lake and the players slipped and slithered towards their summer break.

I'd asked the Norwich studio to make a recording: this, after all, was to be my big breakthrough – a glittering moment from a show-reel that would surely propel me to commentary stardom. But my words were merely evaporating into the ether, for no recording was made. Disaster for me, but the world had been saved from a third-rate Motson clone.

Three years later, after visiting almost every football commentary box in the country as a producer for BBC Radio, I was back in Norwich working for BBC East television and fending off allegations from Suffolk that I was biased towards Norwich – which I probably was, and still am.

My wife and I now live on the M40 corridor, but we love returning to Norfolk. Last time I was at Carrow Road, City beat Manchester United 2–0 and hopes of Premiership survival were on the up. Now that's gone, but I'm just as happy watching the windsurfers on Brancaster beach.

Chapter 9
Share and share alike
David Clayton —————————

I t's a ski slope! That's the best way to describe a graph of virtually any radio station's listening figures. The number of people tuned in climbs steeply at the start of the day, usually peaking during the breakfast shows. Then, as someone indelicately put it, the audience decays during the day. That explains why we, and the other BBC local radio stations in the Eastern Counties join together in the evenings to share programmes.

This wasn't always the case. In its very early days, BBC Radio Norfolk would join Radio 2 at various times during the day and through the evening. This practice is called – and here comes a bit of radio jargon – a 'sustaining service'.

During the eighties Arnold Miller, who was in charge of the BBC TV and radio in Norwich, came up with the idea that we should join up regionally, and share some evening programmes. It had been tried in the East Midlands during the afternoons, when BBC Radio Nottingham made its programme, hosted by the late Dennis McCarthy, available to BBC Radio Derby, Leicester and Lincolnshire. Arnold was then the programme organiser at Nottingham, so was used to the idea.

BBC Radio Norfolk is one of six local radio stations in the Eastern Counties region – the geographical area covered by the *Look East* television programme. The other five are BBC Radio Suffolk in Ipswich, BBC Essex in Chelmsford, BBC Three Counties in Luton covering Bedfordshire, Hertfordshire and Buckinghamshire, BBC Radio Cambridgeshire in Cambridge and BBC Radio Northampton. It's a big region, but already joined together by the regional television service.

The regional programmes make economic sense, because there are less radio listeners about in the evenings when television viewing takes over. Television's viewing figures are just the opposite of radio's – a reverse ski slope if you like.

Les Woodland: Tour de Norfolk

BBC Radio Norfolk has played a big part in hosting these regional programmes. One of the first to have a go from the Norfolk studios was Adrian Finighan, who came to Radio Norfolk from Radio Broadland and soon found he was broadcasting to a much bigger area, covering Cambridge and Peterborough as well as Norfolk. When BBC Radio Suffolk came on air he was heard there too. Adrian geared his show towards a younger teenage audience and even came up with an on-air solution to homework problems. If you were stuck on a maths question, you could call in and if Adrian didn't know the answer, other listeners might have the solution. Adrian involved quite a few youngsters on air with his show and they took charge of the phone-in lines. It was a great grounding in the radio business and some of Adrian's protégés have ended up in various branches of the media.

Les Woodland hosted the mid-week evening regional programme for a while. He was an experienced presenter and journalist working on BBC Radio Cambridgeshire, but lived in Norfolk near Wymondham. Les provided a quirky mix of talking points for the audience to join in with on the phone lines. He is now a writer specialising in cycling books.

Next up was Paul Barnes, whose arrival was, in a way, a happy accident. At the time Paul was a busy regional journalist and presenter on Anglia Television. His partner is Helen McDermott and despite Helen being one of the best known faces on Anglia TV, I rang her to see if she wanted to do some radio programmes on the BBC to cover Keith Skipper's absence on holiday. Keith was, and still is, such a distinctive broadcaster, so when he was on holiday it was difficult to find

Golden opportunity: Paul Barnes

someone with an equally memorable style. Helen was not available, but she suggested Paul might like to have a go on BBC Radio Norfolk. Given his radio credentials – he had been the first reporter on Radio 1's *Newsbeat*, as well as having had a spell working on the *Today* programme on Radio 4 – he was a good choice and enjoyed his fortnight in Keith's *Dinnertime* chair.

It was felt the time was right for a change on the evening programme. Given Paul's obvious empathy with the bigger region from his work at Anglia, he was offered five nights a week on the late regional show. This he did for a few years, but then took one summer off to do some filming for television, and that was where broadcasting legend, Keith Skues, came in to fill the temporary gap. That, too, was a happy accident.

Earlier, in 1993, the Royal Air Force had celebrated its 75th anniversary, and chose RAF Marham, one of the country's most famous combat airfields, as the host base for the celebration, with the Queen in attendance. BBC Radio Norfolk decided the event was well worth covering, so Tony Mallion was sent to produce the outside broadcast. There he encountered a Squadron Leader Skues, who turned out to be Keith Skues, the former Radio 1 and pirate radio broadcaster. Keith was a member of the RAF Reserve and had been called up for some press officer duties at the Marham event.

Back in the Radio Norfolk studios in Norwich, I remember hearing Tony describing the meeting when we were communicating down the OB line off-air, but then forgot about the encounter. However, a few days later, I found myself on the North Lynn Industrial Estate in King's Lynn, where Radio Norfolk was holding a reception to open new studios. Carol Bundock presented a show from there to mark the opening, as the 'great and good' of West Norfolk milled around sipping cocktails. I was on assistant editor duty, handing out drinks and nibbles, and wandered up to Ed Bulpitt from RAF Marham.

Ed said, 'Can I introduce you to Squadron Leader Skues?'

I shook his hand and would not have registered the connection, but for the fact that Skues' voice boomed out a polite reply. I recall asking the man with the dulcet tones, 'Good heavens, you're not *the* Keith Skues?'

I then abandoned circulating round the invited guests to gossip with one of my own personal broadcasting heroes about pirate radio, Radio 1 and the like. At some point the conversation turned to what Keith was doing now. Apart from some temporary RAF duties, it turned out to be not much. Keith had been running Radio Hallam in Sheffield, but that had come to an end and apart from finishing off his *Pop Went the Pirates* book, Keith was a free agent. I offered him a one-off

Pirate of the North Sea, Keith Skues

bank holiday programme, which Keith accepted, and then I panicked. What if Keith Salmon, the editor of Radio Norfolk, thought it a bad idea? No worries – on hearing the proposition, Keith Salmon said he thought Keith Skues was a superb broadcaster, so the deal was done. One programme led to another. Keith stood in for Paul Barnes during his summer break and established himself regionally, then took over from Paul permanently to present the late regional share programme five nights a week for nearly a decade.

Another old pirate also occupied the regional airwaves from Norfolk for a while. Tom Edwards presented a Sunday-night show, but this was at the time of his now well publicised battle with drink, and sadly the show came to an end. Tom won his battle with the bottle and occasionally presents shows on BBC Radio Norfolk. The courage he showed and the affection for him locally mean he's always welcome on Norfolk's airwaves.

Paul Barnes wallows in his *Gold for Grownups* music programme at weekends and I spent a good few years on the Sunday-night regional show myself.

Norfolk's studios also hosted some of the pioneering *Night Shift* programmes during 2002 and 2003 with Keith Greentree, Stephen Bumfrey and Dave Brown. In 2004 Nick Lawrence took over the 7–10 pm programme from Norfolk's studios in The Forum, having come from BBC Three Counties, where he used to present their breakfast show.

Keith Greentree: on the nightshift

Many presenters have graced the Norfolk airwaves from afar, with shows originating from other local radio stations in the region: Richard Spendlove, Steve Madden, Steve Riches, Mark Whall, Sue Marchant, Jon Gaunt, Big George, Liz Mullen, Nick Risby, Andy Peebles and even the late great John Peel.

Although the best presenters try and talk to just one person, it's a sobering thought when you consider the Eastern Countries region is about a fifth of England. People call in from as far as London and Birmingham and the majority of the programmes have been hosted from Norfolk's busy radio studios.

Where are they now?
Adrian Finighan

When I arrived at Radio Norfolk I was concerned that the station may have had a problem with a pilferer. I had never worked for the BBC before, and was alarmed to find everything from broadcast equipment to cutlery and even paper cups stamped 'BBC'. I never did discover the truth behind the rumour that both Roy Waller and Wally Webb have been there so long that they're stamped too. I don't think anyone's going to nick them now, after all this time, do you?

I have such fond memories of my time at the old Norfolk Tower. None of this digital or computer technology nonsense back then – things were reassuringly steam driven and stuck together with gaffer tape. Mind you, Skipper would moan like stink about anything remotely new or hi-tech even then, so goodness knows what he makes of the station's new home at The Forum.

It was – and I'm assured still is – such a friendly place to work. Being there so early on in my career, I was probably too young to appreciate just how lucky I was to be a part of it. I rather took for granted the fact that Radio Norfolk's audience is huge, very loyal and welcomes new voices like old friends. It also contributes with great enthusiasm to any competition, event or appeal that the station may organise. I was made to feel at home right away.

Ah, yes. Those were the days: playing football in the office with Roy Waller and Malcolm Robertson – or cricket in the summer – the rickety old radio car full of half-eaten sandwiches, empty crisp packets, crumbs and, bizarrely, sand. There were the big clunky tape machines that would take your finger off if you weren't careful. I remember the delight of being mothered by Maggie Secker, who was obviously worried that the young Finighan, far from his own mum in Wales, wasn't eating enough or looking after himself properly.

I remember waiting eagerly outside the kitchen with Waller for the moment when the lady from Eastern Gas required 'tasters' to make appreciative noises for her mid-morning broadcast, and dear old Don Shepherd puffing away on his pipe with a look of pure contentment on his face as the sounds of a bygone musical age blasted out of the stereo system in the record library. And, oh of course, records! Thousands of them, stacked from floor to ceiling in the old 'gram' library as it was called, and many a happy hour spent with Lyn McKinney listening to the latest releases at high volume – and being told off by the manager for having it up too loud. No wonder I'm slightly deaf these days, it's all Lyn's fault!

A couple of outside broadcasts are worth mentioning: I became Radio Norfolk's *Flying Eye* traffic reporter for the Norfolk Show one year, but the weather was so awful that I spent the whole time feeling very sick. My reports must have sounded quite odd as the little plane was bounced around in

That was then, this is now: Present day Adrian

the sky above the showground. Imagine someone talking to you from a roller-coaster and you've got it.

'Traffic building up now on all the whoaaa, ug, er, um, approach roads and, ooff, urgh, the A47 looking a bit euaargh, busy,' or something like that.

Then there was the evening spent broadcasting live from Yarmouth on a late summer evening that was so cold that we might as well have been in Siberia. Slurred speech and chattering teeth made most of the broadcast unintelligible. I may not actually have been in Siberia, but it probably sounded like we were all speaking Russian for all the sense we made.

And then there was the outside broadcast that wasn't an outside broadcast at all. With help from a BBC sound effects record, we went up and down the Broads on a cruiser during one programme without leaving the studio and were inundated with calls from listeners who'd come out to meet us, but couldn't find us. I can't remember why we did that. Perhaps it was April Fool's Day!

These days I'm presenting on BBC News 24, or the BBC's international channel, BBC World – look out for me next time you're away on holiday! I also crop up, every now and again, reading the news on Radio 2. So, I've managed to go from Britain's most successful local station to its most successful national one, but, despite the star names, huge audience and central London studios, it just isn't the same. Give me good old Radio Norfolk any day!

Chapter 10

Goodbye to the tower
Lyn McKinney

We're saying goodbye to the tower
Where we broadcast to you, by the hour,
Where the parking was easy,
Though a tiny bit squeezey,
And the space on the end held the power.

Farewell to the kitchen, where in generous mood
Broadcasting chefs offered sumptuous food,
While in pigeon holes nesting,
Listeners' letters, requesting
A greeting, a note, seldom rude.

The office where 'Sir' delivered his roastings
And would-be employees applied for their postings,
A fridge filled with wine
Untouched most of the time,
Except for occasional toastings.

The men, who were caught unawares,
They could stroll to the loo – no one cared,
But for girls on the run
It's not been great fun,
Setting records, by leaping the stairs.

To the studios, we say au revoir,
Where we sweated and toiled by the hour.
The music we played,
The chat we conveyed
And predicted the odd passing shower.

No helipad at Norfolk Tower

How I've cursed Surrey Street, it's true.
It's the road that cut us in two.
No more dodging the weather,
We'll all be together
Behind glass, just like at the zoo.

Rest assured, we'll be on our mettle.
It won't take us long to get settled.
We salute the tower block,
Turn the key in the lock.
Did someone remember the kettle?

As the end of our stay draws nearer,
The future looks brighter and clearer.
Our home, yes, it's changing,
But we're just re-arranging
For the dawn of a sparkling new era.

Chapter 11
The Move

Tim Bishop ———
Head of Regional and Local Programmes, BBC East

Today Radio Norfolk is at the heart of Norwich's futuristic Forum library and learning complex, but that's not how the station's life started. For over 40 years the BBC's Norwich home was in the delightful St Catherine's Close, once a rambling family home, but transformed behind the sweeping staircase and elegant chandeliers of its entrance into a rabbit warren of editing suites, studios and offices. Regional radio lived there and when local radio started, the natural instinct of the BBC was to cram in the newcomer, but there was no room.

The BBC is organised by divisions, and around the country the birth of local radio reinforced the divisive nature of that structure, and was fuelled by it. Radio editors looked to get as far away as possible from their much resented, and better funded, television big sister. Former head of centre, Arnold Miller, summed this up:

> Amazingly, those instructed to identify premises for the new Radio Norfolk were not required to find somewhere near to the existing BBC East building at St Catherine's Close. In Nottingham, the BBC radio and television stations were about a mile apart, and in Devon, radio went to Exeter while television was in Plymouth. Something similar could have happened in Norwich. The fact that they ended as neighbours was a mixture of chance, the height of Norfolk Tower (good for contact with radio cars) and a bit of common sense on the part of the man searching the city – but not policy.

Television quietly sneered at the newcomer, just as network centres sneered at the antics of their regional cousins. Former BBC correspondent, Martin Bell, well remembers when the then director general, Hugh Greene, happened to see the infant *Look East* on a visit to a relative in Bury St Edmunds. In no time at all a senior producer from London was despatched to tell the country cousins how it should be done. In the same way regional television regarded local radio as in some way inferior.

In return, radio veered between a healthy 'nobody loves us, we don't care' cheerful flouting of the ingrained rules of the corporation to create a technological and broadcasting revolution – a defiant attitude that sustains it to this day – and a self-pitying inferiority, complex in its darker moments.

So no one in radio was too unhappy that the new set-up would not fit into the regional headquarters, although they did welcome the tea trolley, laden with cakes, that clattered across the road every day from the nearby and well loved BBC canteen. The choice of Norwich's tallest building made sense, as a wide variety of essential equipment grew steadily across the roof of Norfolk Tower. Initially no one cared very much about the roof space. Later costs jumped into the thousands, as the mobile phone and communications revolution made the high points of the city intensely desirable to a wide variety of companies. A jungle of satellite and phone masts eventually festooned the roof.

At the start local radio created, and was made possible by, an unsung revolution. To quote Arnold Miller again:

> The design of the first BBC local radio stations was, inevitably, influenced by established working radio routines up to then. Thus a presenter in his studio was 'driven' by an operator in a control room the other side of a triple-glazed glass window, perhaps with other station assistants to operate additional equipment like grams or tape machines. The first local stations had two such studios, one 'live', and the second reserved for longer form pre-recorded work, features, documentaries and educational output.
>
> Two things changed all this. First of all local radio rapidly evolved its own programme formats and preferred working patterns, and recognised early on that 'self-op' working was more efficient, more

effective and cheaper. In the end, pressing your own buttons is easier and quicker than telling someone else, and hoping they are prompt. Secondly, all these sound-treated rooms were expensive to build.

When it came to the new phase of stations, of which Norfolk was the first, there was no money for a Studio 2. Instead there were two self-operated areas, but the design nodded in the direction of possible larger-scale productions by offering a larger studio area between the two, which either or both could control.

Wally Webb and Iain Nicholson

Radio presenters cued their own music and opened the microphones for their own guests. Not the way it's usually done at the BBC, but cheap, effective and instrumental in allowing local radio to roll out across the country at low cost.

In Norfolk many floors down from its rooftop aerials, the station was at least all on one floor. But the giant L of the ground floor of the building had other disadvantages that would only become a real Achilles' heel in later years.

The pavement frontage became the centre of the station, with a newsroom and office filled initially with the friendly clattering of typewriters and then by the ceaseless tapping of computer keyboards, alongside the regular games of office cricket. Reception occupied the elbow of the L, with the lavatories off to one side and the management down the back corridor.

The giant studio block dominated the long L of the building. When they were built, the studios were seen as havens of peace and isolation from the bustle of the office or the world. Studios were vast constructions with walls sound-proofed with traditional materials and to levels of resilience no one would consider necessary these days. As a result, when the

Norfolk Airline took over in October 1983 and produced a need for a bigger studio, moving a wall to create a marginally bigger space became an essential, but expensive and difficult exercise. Arnold Miller:

> In reality this 'middle studio' was under-used, while the two smaller self-op cubicles were busy and overcrowded. The suggestion was made to move one wall further into the centre space, thereby making a much larger self-op cubicle for all the main sequences at breakfast and so on, while leaving a centre space big enough for answering phones, setting up live response, briefing guests etc. It seemed a good idea, and gained rapid approval.
>
> Moving these walls is not as simple as it sounds. To achieve 'sound separation' – that is, keeping out all the noise you don't want, as well as providing a good acoustic – these were 'double Camden' walls, which in effect meant a total of ten or eleven structural layers separated by a middle gap. What we hadn't realised was that the chosen wall also contained lots of electrical gear for studio kit, lights, air conditioning ...

Gone home: a rare empty production office

Costs multiplied and tempers frayed, but in the end the wall was moved.

The history of modern management is reflected in the changes made over the 25 years that the BBC occupied the building. At first, grand offices were built for the engineer in charge, the programme organiser and, of course, the largest office of all was created for the managing editor, complete with the obligatory and well stocked fridge full of drinks.

By the time the station was thinking about moving, all of those trappings felt from another world. A scheme to sell off the management corridor was hamstrung by the fact the station would be left with no access to the lavatories. Over the years the difficulties of getting through two security-coded doors and back into the studio, during a record or the news, had left more than one embarrassed presenter.

As the lease on Norfolk Tower ran down, the BBC was thinking about moving. St Catherine's Close had many virtues, but it was riddled with asbestos and the wiring needed radical attention to fit out the station for the digital age. Neither building would comply easily with new legislation on disabled access. Needs had changed. Moving to a single building offered a big financial saving, as the new equipment would need far less studio and technical space.

The calm exterior of the old BBC buildings had concealed frenetic activity, but remained a viewer-free zone, partly because of cold-war thinking. In any well run coup, the seizing of the radio station is the key moment, so the BBC had seen its transmitters and buildings as vulnerable and to be protected first and foremost. Regional buildings were discreet, secure and anonymous, each with an antique safe stuffed full of moth-eaten and now worthless instructions about how to cope with nuclear attack. Some of those concerns are back today, with the more selective and arbitrary threat of terrorism, but the desire to be clearly open for business in an organisation funded by the public is far more important. The BBC cannot hide away in fear.

The old philosophy had created a problem. In Norfolk, 'Where's the BBC?' you'd ask. 'Blarst me, I think it's somewhere near Bonds [now John Lewis]', would come the uncertain reply. No one needed to ask where Anglia was. The former Agricultural Hall remains one of the landmark buildings of the city.

Across the country the BBC wanted the licence-fee payers to be able to see, visit and drop in to use the organisation that they pay for. High-profile city-centre buildings were now the order of the day – and not just any high profile buildings. With concerns over the state of British architecture ringing in their ears, the leaders of the BBC felt that the UK's key cultural organisation should make a contribution. In its time Broadcasting House in London, with its Eric Gill sculptures, had been iconic. Since then, British design had lived through the dire architecture of the 1960s. What buildings would this generation leave behind that people would look at and be excited by? Could the BBC be part of a design revolution, in line with a modern Britain not ignoring the past, but very much looking forward.

The search for a new building in Norwich began alongside similar searches in Glasgow, Birmingham, Hull and other cities and towns across Britain. Local radio had long been the poor relation. but this time it was going to be different. Greg Dyke was then the director general and he wanted buildings that would make bold statements.

Interviewing the DG, Greg Dyke in Norfolk

Birmingham moved from the shabby sprawling homely Pebble Mill to the bright upmarket Mailbox. Staff worried about the loss of canteens, parking and the broadcast heritage of the building. 'We used to make *Pebble Mill at One* here,' one told him. That, and a complaint about lack of parking, convinced him that moving would help to change the culture of the organisation. He urged staff now not to dwell on what used to happen, but to look forward to new programmes and new opportunities.

Years before, the BBC had considered moving out of Norwich to somewhere more central to the region. Cambridge had seemed a natural home, somewhere off the new A14, the central highway of the region. That scheme hadn't happened, but as the search for suitable sites meandered on, looking beyond Norwich once again began to seem a serious option, with leases due to expire and no suitable site emerging.

Head of programmes David Holdsworth had grown frustrated with the process, and in 2002 the local management began the business of enlisting what help there was. New city council chief executive, Anne Seex, was just getting to know Norwich. She was lobbied by the BBC, and then headed off to the Forum Trust, where she represented the council.

In 1994, Norwich's sixties' library had burnt down. There was regret for the books and records lost, but few could find it in their heart to miss the building. Until, that is, it became clear how difficult it would be to fund a new one. For years the library languished in an old furniture showroom on Ber Street.

The city rallied and, with the help of the Millennium Lottery fund and the cooperation of both city and county councils – not something for which they are traditionally renowned – the idea for The Forum emerged. Architect, Sir Michael Innes, designed a thoroughly modern and unique building that would reflect the historic St Peter Mancroft Church in its vast glass frontage. As well as the library, it was to contain restaurants and a learning centre, and was eventually also to house the tourist information centre and the Origins tourist attraction. However The Forum needed other tenants to pull in sufficient rent to make the project work – and not just any tenants – organisations that would fulfil the building's purpose.

The Forum had space; the BBC needed a building. The two were not talking, but could there, Anne wondered, be an arranged marriage? Meantime, long-serving and well liked Norwich city councillor and head of economic development Harry Watson had been to America and seen the exciting broadcasting headquarters of worldwide news channel CNN – in a shopping mall. This set him thinking. As the idea for locating the BBC in The Forum gathered momentum, he became an enthusiastic supporter, quietly helping to make the project work. Councillors step into the limelight and take the flak for all sorts of things. They do not get paid, but they do give their time, often for the good of the city and not just for party political advantage. It doesn't always make the headlines,

131

but it's the sort of day-to-day activity that really makes things happen.

The question then was: would the BBC and The Forum be able to fit together as library and a broadcast centre? Forum innovations man, John Smith, felt it started as a shotgun marriage, but then he started thinking. What is a library? A place where people come for information, a place where they come to be entertained and a place that helps with education. There could be a fit with the long-running aims of the BBC to inform, to educate and to entertain. As libraries had begun to deal more and more in electronic information, the two seemed to be moving closer. The only difference was that the BBC exists to broadcast. Both shared a sense of public value and public purpose.

Yet there was a mountain of problems to overcome. The Forum was half-built and the available space was simply not big enough. As David Holdsworth put it:

> The Forum offered to build a second building, but as we thought about it, the notion of two sites, even with an aerial walkway between them, felt exactly the opposite of what we wanted. At one time the BBC had four sites. Now we wanted everyone in the same place, so that online, television and radio worked in the same area, enabling each to benefit from the other.

The Forum management thought about it and offered to shift their entire offices to the second building. Greg Dyke became the first director general to visit Norwich and liked it. The deal was done. But for project manager Paul Baker, a television director, the problems were just beginning:

> I'd spent over ten years coping with the stresses of directing live news programmes, breaking stories, technical problems and the occasional personality clash. None of that fully prepared me for sorting out the single most difficult problem in our move into The Forum. The move involved dozens of contractors for all manner of works from fixing signs to installing a state-of-the-art television studio and transmission

Up front: BBC Radio Norfolk at The Forum

system I'd become fluent in the jargon of digital television, radio, webpage design and desk finishes. I'd worked through the night trying to make the television gallery work for the first *Look East* pilots.

All of that was a piece of cake compared to my biggest challenge: the front door. Our front door had to do four things: be opened by staff at any time of day or night; be able to be locked securely; work as a fire exit and open automatically for disabled people. To ensure this would happen correctly, we employed an expert in automated door design, an expert in electronic locks and an expert in fire doors. Unfortunately, they didn't seem to have talked to each other. Things wouldn't close. Then the doors opened spontaneously, in the middle of the night. The climax was when the doors started flapping – opening and closing repeatedly, like a tent door flapping in the wind. And it always seemed to happen just as I was about to go home at the end of a long day or at the weekend.

After two months of this, I was on first-name terms with the various repairmen. They all blamed each other. I decided the only way to solve this was for all four contractors who had worked on the various parts of the doors to come to Norwich at the same time. I was tingling with happy expectation when they all arrived at 9 am. I explained the problems to them and left them to fix it once and for all. At 10.30 am, I returned to hear their verdict. Each one said their part of the door was working perfectly. Excellent, I thought, and asked what they had replaced.

'Oh, nothing,' they chorused, 'it's all working.' My happy expectation tingles were being replaced with rumbles of frustration. The doors were not working before they had arrived. They all agreed. They had done nothing. They all agreed. They said the doors would now work. I did not agree.

I pointed out there was something missing – such as any single action or repair that might have changed anything. They then – and only then – accepted that I might have a point. I left them to it and decided I had met my match. I could handle any catastrophe in live television, but could I manage an open door? No.

Stewart White, first on air at the new Forum studios

Delays hit the television equipment, so it was agreed radio would move first. Thousands of miles of wiring and cabling were installed and tested. And first on air, ironically, was Norfolk Saturday morning presenter and *Look East* presenter Stewart White. A tired but determined group just had to be there for the first broadcast.

A whole new philosophy and technology had transformed the isolated studios of Norfolk Tower days into an open airy construction that the public could see live on air and was open to the world, changing the feel of radio, but still allowing presenters to create their own intimate world when necessary. As The Forum went live, Paul Baker remembers:

> One of the considerations was the transparency of the building. The interior of the old building was beautifully shielded from the public gaze of our audience. Presenters could be as casual or unkempt as they wanted. When we came to discussing who should sit where, there were some slightly unexpected concerns. You'd imagine presenters would be keen to be seen, but we discovered there are exceptions and limits. Some presenters (Roy Waller) were wary about sitting next to the floor-to-ceiling glass walls, and (Stewart) being visible in the radio studios. Now these are people who adore their audience ... but had been so used to the visibility being one-way and controlled. Not any more. I'm happy to say that some of them can still be caught playing air guitar, momentarily ignoring the glass windows and the public gaze.

Television followed and The Forum became home. Has it changed us? Yes in all sorts of ways. When Norwich City's victory parade for winning the Championship and heading for the Premiership was held, The Forum and the BBC were at the centre of the story. *Look East* presenter Stewart White, on the balcony of City Hall, was introducing Delia Smith live to a cheering crowd that spread across the road to The Forum. Those who couldn't see directly could watch on a big screen outside at the front.

The staff had had lots of worries: about the loss of a

canteen and of car parking, fears of the changes and concerns about the space. As one of their union officials emerged on that night, he looked around and said quietly, 'I suppose you think this makes it all worthwhile.'

And yes it does. The public owns the BBC. Thousands of them have now been able to visit it, take part in an event at The Forum or simply walk by and watch some radio being made. Everyone knows where the BBC is. Everyone pays for it, so they have a right to know.

Where are they now?
Sylvie Waller

I was first employed by the BBC after Radio Norfolk had been opened just a few months. A friend of mine who I worked with at Air Anglia, Jill Mackintosh, got one of the first posts, and after a couple of months, contacted me to say that they were looking for temporary staff. As they say, the rest is history.

I was known as the most permanent 'temp' on the station. In time I became a member of staff and worked for most departments of Radio Norfolk, finally ending up working alongside Roy Waller for a great number of years.

One of my happiest experiences while working for BBC Radio Norfolk was when they decided to send Roy and me to visit a gas rig 90 miles out in the North Sea to present our programme from there. We were flown out from the Bacton gas terminal, from where we rig-hopped until we eventually got to our Amoco platform. I remember looking out at what looked like a postage stamp on which we were to land. We spent two days with the guys on this rig – I was given the best room with a proper bed! Roy was put in with the roustabouts. We had the most amazing food, and this memory will stay with me forever.

Then there was the memorable BBC holiday, when Roy and I, plus Jill Bennett and Trevor Austin – who used to run the King's Lynn office – took a party of Radio Norfolk listeners to the Canadian Rockies. Unbeknown to me, Roy asked the captain of the rather large cruise ship we were travelling on to marry us on board. He loved the idea, but declined because he had never carried out a wedding ceremony. Instead, he arranged for us to get married during our next stopover, which was at town called Kamloops in the province of British Colombia – and happened to be for three days, the length of time needed in one place before a wedding could be held. It was taken out of our hands and all the arrangements were made. We were married secretly on 23 June 1991 in the Honeymoon Suite of the Stockman's Hotel. None of the listeners who were travelling with us believed Roy when we told them at breakfast the next day! That evening they were all invited to the reception in the hotel ballroom – and the champagne flowed.

It's a date: Sylvie and Roy Waller

Rodeo Roy and Sylvie

I made many good friends over my many years at the BBC, some of whom will be my friends always. I left two years ago and now very much lead the life of a lady 'who does lunch'. I love my life and can now meet all the people that working fulltime did not allow. When I left the BBC, Roy bought me a new car – the registration is AGO and he says it stands for 'Always Going Out'. Our house, by the way, is called 'Kamloops'.

Chapter 12
The website
Peter Cook

New technology is a part of life at BBC Radio Norfolk. Gone are the days when reporters carried around a Uher portable tape recorder, the size of an encyclopaedia. Today our choice of recording equipment is about the size of a mobile phone. The fax was a major stride forward in the delivery of fast news, as the latest press release churned out from the machine in the corner. Now with the advent, some might say scourge, of email we rarely use it.

The vinyl record was first replaced by compact discs and now we play our music from a computer. Cut fingers, caused by a carelessly wielded razor blade, as producers made some last minute edits to that all important interview, are a thing of the past. Today a click on a computer screen does the same job.

We have always been fast to grab a new piece of technology too. During the last general election, we trialled a new reporter link using a mobile phone. We've broadcast from the Gulf using a small hand-held piece of kit, and taken the entire breakfast show to Normandy, using a piece of technology not too far removed from a normal telephone line.

A decade ago we didn't have any idea of the impact text-messaging could have on us or our listeners, but Radio Norfolk was the first station to introduce it. Within nine months we had received a quarter of a million messages.

Of course, there are those of us who have taken time to come to terms with the new technology at our fingertips, but have come to enjoy it. Presenter John Mills well remembers that first step into the world of the web:

> My initial feelings about emails were along the lines of 'step back in amazement', closely followed by a fear that the whole world of letter-writing and postal delivery was now in jeopardy. But then I read an article

which suggested that we were really moving back to the Victorian age, when five or more postal deliveries a day encouraged a vigorous and effective correspondence. That persuaded me of the civilising effect that this new technology might offer. Indeed, even with the scam and spam problems that have emerged, I still revel in the fact that I can provide instant email response – and that probably goes for the recipient, who might otherwise wait forever for my reply!

Others spotted the potential straight away. Wally Webb was keen to get his hands on this new way of communicating with our listeners:

> I remember seeing my first ever email at the home of the then news editor Ian Hyams. He was using it to keep in touch with his sibling in America and I was immediately struck by the system that would wait for you to log on and then deliver the correspondence, after which I couldn't wait to get onto the internet myself.
>
> As for studio work, it was probably *Sunday Requests* that started to get emails in any volume. I know listeners were asking me for an email address even before the BBC had got one sorted. What is remarkable is that it is the older listeners who seem to have embraced that technology quickest to use as a tool for communicating with us.
>
> When the webcams came, I thought we would have to be on our best behaviour all the time, but remarkably you tend not to even think about it. Maybe it would be different if it were a live stream.

The internet has been one of the most important technological changes to reach us in the past 10 years. Today it's commonplace for a reporter to tap away on their keyboard to find that all-important piece of background information. Of course, BBC Radio Norfolk has found its own home there too.

Former reporter Stephen Lee well remembers his efforts to put us on the information super-highway during 1995:

Super-highway for Norfolk: reporter Stephen Lee

The computer department rigged up a wobbly connection to the world wide web and suddenly a few of us got our first ever email addresses. But who to write to? The only people we knew with email addresses were ourselves!

Searching for a web page was a long-drawn-out affair. No pictures, only text – which took an age to display on screen. But even with those first tentative steps, we realised a little of the enormous impact the internet could have and decided we needed to connect with our audience this way.

The internet was seen as a hobby for computer nerds and therefore the corporation's offering was the BBC Networking Club. We approached them to see if we could publish some information about Radio Norfolk on the web. The designers set to work – and suddenly, there we were, the first BBC local radio station to have their very own web pages. By today's standards they weren't much, for the only picture was our logo and the rest was a few pages of simple text. The content didn't go much further than our programme schedules and a little bit of the station's history. But from small acorns, big oaks grow and we were on our way.

We mentioned our new website and email address on air, not quite knowing what to expect. But it wasn't long before our first emails arrived; there really were listeners out there with computers. Those early emails were met with much excitement. Gradually, as time went on, more and more people began to contact us over the internet and our pages grew. We toured the building and persuaded our presenters to pose for a photo to put on the site. Listeners began sending us what's ons and dedications by email. Senior BBC management saw what we were doing, and we were invited to London to give a seminar on how the internet could be used as a massive research tool. I remember some were enthused, while others were sceptical about the range and accuracy of online information.

Being first with something can sometimes lead you into trouble, and it wasn't long before the BBC hierarchy spotted our attempts at reaching out through the internet and ordered us to remove our own website as the corporation embarked on a programme of new sites across the country.

The first crude, but effective website

Presenter Graham Barnard valued the crude, but effective site we treasured:

> I remember being very proud of us for taking the initiative to come up with our own website, and even more proud when it emerged that we really shouldn't be doing it any more. The BBC's local radio station websites were starting to emerge, and we all knew that one day our pioneering site would have to close. But there was a feeling that it would stay on-line for as long as possible. The 'do different' in Norfolk attitude was shining through!

And so, the plug was pulled. But a new more dynamic, more user friendly – more professional website was to emerge. Norfolk, one step ahead as always, was to be one of the first counties to have a local BBC website. Martin Barber, our senior website producer, was there at the birth of the new site:

> When the website launched it was an incredibly exciting time. Some six months in development, bbc.co.uk/norfolk was launched in October 2000. For the first time editorial, created by a BBC online team of three in Norfolk, became available to a global audience. It was also a time when the BBC in Norfolk

was meeting the needs of a new and younger audience. In addition to news, sport and weather – the BBC's core services – audiences in Norfolk could engage in the areas of music, clubbing and the arts. The multimedia environment of the internet allowed us to bring new coverage of the visual arts in the county, and showcase new talent from local animators and film makers, in addition to the written word.

There's always been some confusion about bbc.co.uk/norfolk and BBC Radio Norfolk. The *Where I Live* site is not an online version of the radio station. There is some common ground in areas of news and sport, at times of emergency like school closures information and being there when things begin to go wrong. The horrendous winter storms were just one occasion the BBC Norfolk website provided a dialogue and access to the emergency services – the people of Norfolk airing their views via the website's message boards, for the service providers to respond.

Where I Live website circa October 2004

BBC Norfolk website updated September 2001

The world of bbc.co.uk/norfolk has undergone major redevelopments at least once every 12 months since the site began. From how the site looks to the way it is produced, the changes reflect the growth in internet use, the higher technical specifications in people's homes and offices and better delivery methods. With more and more users enjoying access to the internet via broadband, the more we've been able to deliver video and audio on demand – including live streaming of BBC Radio Norfolk.

The website, in just five years, has also become a valuable archive of local content, capturing those important moments in the county's history, to be enjoyed many years into the future – for example, the joyous celebrations of Norwich City's promotion to the Premiership in 2004.

Hundreds of photographs and exclusive video of that happy time will be kept online for fans to enjoy for years to come. Or it could be the incredible pictures of the spring tides in 2005 – a night when the Norfolk coast went onto high alert, when online pictures of the night provided not only a valuable view of events in the county at the time, but also for people in the future.

As the site has developed, so have the expectations and contributions of our users. More and more people in the county are now writing their own features for bbc.co.uk/norfolk and enjoying the thrill of having their work published – from the online diaries of Norfolk people adventuring to far-flung corners of the world to stories of life at home. From photo galleries and special projects like *This Norfolk Life*, to debates on our message boards, *Video Nation*, *Blast* and sharing a faith – the BBC Norfolk website has opened a new door to the people of Norfolk to share their voice and the rich tapestry of life that is woven throughout the county.

The website has had its share of firsts in its short life. We were proud to host the first mobile webcam the BBC ever used in the UK, mounted on a Broads Authority patrol craft. We've hosted the most successful live webchat to have taken place within the English regions' new media family and who knows what's to come.

The web team is a real part of BBC Radio Norfolk, and those in it have done their creative best to drag us into the twenty-first century – turning studio 1A at Norfolk Tower into a beach complete with sand, a tart's boudoir for Valentine's day (Stewart White was especially fond of that one) and a shrine to Norwich City to celebrate their promotion to the Premiership – all visible on the webcam. With our webcams, we can also transport you all around the county.

Once again Radio Norfolk was at the forefront, when we

put the news hour of our nightly *Drive Live* show online. That was all we could offer for several years, while the BBC negotiated with the record companies for the rights to stream our output, including music. We eventually got the permission we needed, and in November 2004 Radio Norfolk went international. We know from their emails that expatriates like to listen, and we now have listeners calling our phone-ins from across the world.

There've been some memorable moments. There was the show hosted by CBBC presenter Jake Humphrey, which attracted our biggest online audience, and resulted in listeners turning up on the landing outside our studio, peering in to watch Jake and the former Fame Academy star Alistair Griffin perform, while they listened on their portable radios.

Who knows what the future will bring? Whatever it is, I'd like to think BBC Radio Norfolk will be ready to embrace it and make it a part of our successful family. In changing technological times there's one thing for sure – with bbc.co.uk/norfolk – Norfolk will never be far away, no matter where you are in the world.

Where are they now?
Keith Skipper

Of course, when it comes to adventure, travel, wanderlust and unlikely diversions, I leave the rest standing somewhere along the Aylsham bypass. Since my release from Radio Norfolk's Cell 33, a decade ago, my itinerary reads like Jeremy Clarkson's route map to infamy – and that's no mean feat for someone who cannot drive.

I am still suffering from bus-lag after the long haul to Hunstanton, while I travelled from Cromer to Yarmouth 24 times without a ticket – I walked. Then there was that windy day when I climbed Beeston Bump and floated down under a parachute.

'That's very dangerous,' said a Sheringham Sherpa, 'coming down here in a parachute.'

'But I didn't come down in a parachute,' I protested vehemently. 'I went up in a tent.'

Keith taking time out to survey the Castle Mall building site before biking back to Cromer

Keith discovers an interesting reed

In-between times, I produced another 15 books – colouring them all in before teatime – and undertook countless safaris across the Norfolk wastelands to rant, rave and ruminate in broad dialect tones. There were no complaints. No one understood a word.

So I continue on my Marco Polo way, trailblazing and transmitting true culture to darker corners of the Norfolk empire. I'll visit other cinemas when I've mended the puncture, pumped up the tyres and wrapped the sandwiches.

PS What's the difference between a joist and a girder? The first wrote Ulysses and the second wrote Faust.

Chapter 13
The non-technical guide to our transmitters

Graham Barnard —————————————————

Anoraks done up tight now, please! No transmitters, no BBC Radio Norfolk. We have four, which is a bit greedy. It was my pleasure to travel around the county on a miserable summer's day to take pictures of our towers of broadcasting power, so you don't have to.

Let's start in the west, and the West Lynn medium-wave mast, one of the few in Britain that broadcasts on this frequency, so Matthew Gudgin once told me in the *Look East* canteen. I've picked up West Lynn in Dumfries and Galloway. Come on, you have to do something on a wet Sunday evening in Dumfries and Galloway, as beautiful as the countryside is! According to my BBC yearbook for 1982, West Lynn has a power rating of 0.25 kW, about the same as a tenth of an electric kettle. It would take ages to make a cup of tea, if using it as a kettle. You have to admit it's a rather boring mast, but you can see it clearly from throughout King's Lynn, should you want to. There's a radio-car receiver right at the very top, which connects to Norwich via a

West Lynn 873 AM

147

Great Massingham 104.4 FM

Postwick 855 AM

high-quality phone-line. In turn, the transmitter is fed by a separate feed from our studios in Norwich. Are you still awake? Apparently the West Lynn mast stands on marshland, so could sink at any time!

The second mast is a bit more like it. More metal, with a definite mast-ness about it. It's west Norfolk's way of hearing us more clearly on good old VHF. Located on the outskirts of the wonderful village of Great Massingham, it currently broadcasts in mono. Please don't ask why. It gets its signal from Stoke Holy Cross near Norwich. As it's a relay station at the moment, we can't do separate shows for west Norfolk as yet, but we're working on it.

In my BBC yearbook for 1984, its frequency is shown as being 96.7 FM, used these days for another Lynn radio station. So it is on 104.4 FM with mixed polarisation, and radiates at a power of 4.2 kW – about the same power as half an electric shower on the medium setting. You can pick up this transmitter on the moon if you have the right equipment, and stand on one leg while doing so. My mum listens to me via the Great Massingham mast. Nice water tower too.

The third is another dull medium-wave transmitter, I'm afraid, but at least you can pick it up on your fillings or stainless steel sink unit if you're very lucky. Postwick is just outside Norwich, and other medium-wave radio stations (even non-BBC ones) get broadcast from here. There are two masts, with some of the radio stations on one, and the rest on the other. I've received Postwick in Calais, as there's nothing to interrupt the sea crossing. It has a power of 1 kW, so you can make a cup of tea on it four times faster than at West Lynn.

The fourth transmitter is just showing off. Please don't pay it any attention. How lucky must the good folk of Stoke Holy Cross and Poringland be, getting such a marvellous view of this tower! All sorts of radio gets sent out from here, including our 95.1 FM broadcasts, but exactly from where I'm not sure. Let's pretend our actual transmitter is the biggest sticky-out bit.

Stoke Holy Cross 95.1 FM

You'll be fascinated to learn that our 95.1 FM broadcasts used to radiate from the television mast at Tacolneston near Wymondham. However, because our equipment was actually located underground, it was only moles who could receive Radio Norfolk in the early days. They now listen on the internet, as they can't get reception from Stoke Holy Cross. It's so hard to please everyone.

My BBC yearbook for 1984 reported that Tacolneston transmitted Radio Norfolk at a power of 5 point something kW – I assume Stoke Holy Cross does so at the same power. Obviously, 5 point something kW means if you were to wire it up to a kettle, your tea would be made before you'd even filled it with water. It was a very exciting moment in my life when Tacolneston was switched off, and Stoke Holy Cross switched on, immediately improving reception along the Dereham Road in Norwich. I remember it well. It happened during *Norfolk Tonight* one evening at about ten past six, after the news while a record was on.

Where are they now?
Ian Masters

I was involved with the birth of BBC Radio Norfolk even before its conception, as the then BBC controller of local radio, Michael Barton, and I had talked for hours (indeed years) about the need to establish a local station in the county.

I had worked for Michael right from the start of my radio and television career when he asked me to present the three-hour morning news sequence at BBC Radio Sheffield back in 1969. I owe to him and Tim Neale, then programme organiser of Radio Sheffield, just about everything for my 36 years' career in broadcasting.

Even before the BBC promised the money to launch the station, Michael and I went to look at the sort of building that might be suitable. We investigated a high place called Norfolk Tower. Then suddenly it came to be – Norfolk Tower and BBC Radio Norfolk. Appointing new staff. The reality of dreaming new programmes. I was thrilled for them. One of the happiest memories I have is of Michael calling to tell me it was all going to happen.

As far as I was concerned, that was going to be the end to the affair for me. I was a hard-working presenter and broadcast journalist anchoring BBC *Look East* and appearing almost nightly, either live or on film, in the *Nationwide* programme.

Then the new station manager, Mike Chaney, and his programme organiser, Peter Glanville, asked me to have a drink with them – we seemed to do a lot of drinking in those days. They suggested that I might like to present the Saturday and Sunday three-hour early morning shows.

'Just a bit of music and chat – you know the sort of thing.'

'Not bloody likely,' I replied.

'Come on, chum,' said Peter, 'you'd love it.'

'Don't talk daft,' I replied, 'I am already working 12 hours a day for TV, and there's no way I can do it. Sorry.'

Three weeks later on the opening weekend there I was –

and up every Saturday and Sunday at 5am for the next three years. Of course I loved every moment. And the people who manned the station were great. Then the audience came. I could not believe those early audience figures: staggering, flattering and humbling. Oh, yes. Norfolk certainly did need its own local station. To this day I believe it was the best because the community made it so.

After presenting some 8,000 television and radio programmes for the BBC, there came a sad moment – presenting my final show in March 1983. After that I became a boss, first of all as manager of BBC Radio Cambridgeshire, then as head of television for BBC South.

I left the BBC in 1992 and became the controller of broadcasting for the Thomson Foundation. I am still doing that, with a few more months to go before retirement. I now lead a team of highly experienced broadcasting consultants. We constantly travel around the world to countries like India, China and Russia, and in Africa and Eastern Europe, passing on knowledge to help less fortunate broadcasters in the development of democratic broadcasting. A thrilling and privileged existence. But ask me the most thrilling moment of all? Well, I would have to say – switching on the transmitter to broadcast my first show for Norfolk on that brand new radio station a quarter of a century ago.

Piece to camera: the opening of BBC Radio Norfolk

Chapter 14
The Future
Chris Goreham

Coming into BBC Radio Norfolk some 18 years after it launched, meant joining a place where the style of broadcasting was already well defined. Nearly two decades' worth of presenters, producers and management had worked to make the station sound the way that it did.

I have been asked to describe where I was and what I was doing on 11 September 1980, but I can't. It's not my fault; BBC Radio Norfolk first went on air some 20 months before I was born. As far as I'm concerned, BBC Radio Norfolk has always been there. Initially it was the station my grandparents always had on when I went round to their house as a kid. Perhaps that's when the seeds were sewn. I'm not saying I made my career choice as a five-year-old in-between games of Subbuteo and picking up worms in the garden, but being subjected to it from such an early age possibly had such an effect on the subconscious that I was always destined to end up working in Norfolk Tower and then the Forum.

While I was growing up, I thought I was definitely going to be a professional footballer. I loved soccer, and loved Norwich City in particular. Like most boys, I guess, I genuinely believed I would one day be pulling on the yellow and green shirt, and scoring at Carrow Road. But there comes a time in every boy's life when it dawns on you that you are not actually very good at football – or in my case even spectacularly bad. I may have loved playing football, but I never even made the first 11 at Woodland View Middle School in Spixworth. Most teenagers go through a similar thing about becoming the lead singer in a huge band too. That's also a stage I went through but, again, the lack of any sort of musical talent cut short my ambition in that department.

Thankfully, though, all those people who wish they had made it as a darling of the Barclay End still enjoy talking about football. When I worked out you could actually get paid for doing that, there was only one job I wanted. As a 15-year-old at Sprowston High School, I was sent out to look for work experience. Radio Norfolk turned me down on account of my being too young, but I can be quite persuasive and bothered the management sufficiently for them to let me help out on the *Saturday Special* sports show when I turned 16 in 1998.

Eventually sports editor Matthew Gudgin allowed me on the air. I reported from the Wellesley in Great Yarmouth on a Jewson League football match one very cold Saturday. It wasn't the most spectacular of starts to a broadcasting career. The curse of the mobile phone meant most of my

Chris Goreham reflects on another home win

reports were cut short, and I finished up doing my final piece from a lay-by on the Acle Straight in a desperate attempt to get a better phone signal. That pioneering technique of doing football reports with traffic flying by at high speed in the background has never caught on.

People often ask about the best way of 'getting into' radio. I usually reply that there is no set way of finding a job in broadcasting which, I realise, is a really unhelpful answer, but it is true. Everyone's story is different. Some go through university, get degrees and become properly qualified. Others fall into it as a second career. Then there is my route – the 'lucky' way. Here there are no exams – you just hang around the place for no money doing whatever you're asked to do until eventually people trust you enough to let you on the air.

So much of what goes on at Radio Norfolk seems to happen by happy accident. When someone suddenly left for another job in the summer of '98, I was asked to stand in for two weeks, doing the sports news on the breakfast show, while they found someone who was older and probably better qualified. That fortnight became a month, and before I knew it I'd been getting up at 4.15am and talking about football on the radio to Louise Priest and then Graham Barnard on *Today in Norfolk* for five years.

Louise Priest: early starter

As I write this I've just completed 18 months of presenting the 5–7pm drivetime show. Again this was something that came my way by complete fluke. I was always adamant that I didn't really want to do news and that I was only interested in working on the sports desk. But when I was offered a month of presenting *Drive Live*, I thought it would be a good opportunity to get some experience of doing something else. That month has now lasted for a year and a half.

People often talk about the family atmosphere at Radio Norfolk. It sounds like a terrible cliché, but it is actually very true. Where else would a jumped-up 16-year-old have been accepted so openly? In fact, the ultimate example of this family phenomenon occurred within a few weeks of starting on the early sport shift. One morning my dad was a guest on the breakfast show; it was quite a test to do a sports bulletin and follow a parent on the air.

Even in recent months I've seen things that I know just don't happen in any other office. I can't imagine many people, as they go about their daily jobs, have had to dodge a moving Dalek as they try to get back to their desk, but I have, honestly!

I mentioned earlier my complete lack of talent when it comes to sport and yet I've found myself in places I've no real right to be, just because of where I work. Two of the best experiences I've ever had involved piggybacking on the success of Norwich City. One was being asked to watch the 2002 play-off final at the Millennium Stadium from the touchline. It was incredible to be allowed on the pitch before and after the game, and to share in the atmosphere created by the thousands of people who travelled from Norfolk. I also learned that day that it isn't easy to think of sensible questions to ask footballers when they've just been beaten on penalties. The fact that any of them actually agreed to be interviewed was incredible, but they did, even though a few of them were tearful enough to make Gazza look happy.

Then there was the promotion to the Premiership in 2004. Again, despite having played absolutely no part in the success, my BBC pass got me on board the open-top bus as it paraded through the city centre in front of thousands and thousands of people, with the trophy on board. It took all the self-control I could muster not to touch the famous old trophy, but I did just about manage to hold myself back. I have a feeling I rather outstayed my welcome that night, though. I got so carried away with the live broadcasting that I missed the point where the media was supposed to get off the bus and finished up back with the players and their families at the training ground at Colney. Those open-top buses aren't quite such a pleasant experience at 60 mph on the A11.

It's not just football either. Another undoubted highlight was commentating on Norfolk's cricket team when they won the ECB Trophy at Lord's in 2001.

Watching Norfolk play cricket has always been a big passion of the station's sports editor, and Matthew Gudgin really rose to the occasion for that day, securing the services of *Test Match Special*'s Norfolk-born commentator Henry Blofeld and somehow negotiating us the use of the *TMS* commentary box. It was quite something just witnessing Henry Blofeld's famous descriptive powers in action. A thrill, yes, but also quite daunting – he's not the easiest of acts to follow on the air. While he effortlessly picked up the name of every single player on the pitch, I struggled – but I had a children's cricket book hidden away in my bag that day to help me remember the fielding positions. It's not easy telling your silly-mid-offs from your long-ons under pressure.

There's also a certain unpredictability about working for BBC Radio Norfolk, which makes it so attractive. You never quite know what the next caller is going to say on the air and which avenue that might take you down for the rest of whatever programme you're working on. Sometimes, however, it can be your own colleagues who provide that sudden unexpected curveball.

While producing the *Saturday Special* sports programme one day, I took a phone call from Nick Bowler, who was out covering a local cricket match involving Vauxhall Mallards. It was one of the most memorable calls I've taken. Nick explained that he might not be available to do his next report because a 'situation had arisen'. One of the Mallards' players had been injured and they were short of a twelfth man. For reasons that still remain a mystery – perhaps it was just because his surname is cricket related – they pressed Nick into action as a substitute fielder. So rather than covering the game, our man finished up taking a vital catch that they still talk about to this day around the boundary at Brundall – or at least Nick does.

If there's one time local radio really comes into its own, it's when there is extreme weather. It's a subject British people are famous for talking about. As nasty as extreme weather can be, I always get the sense many people quite enjoy the drama that can be caused. There's the image of huddling round the radio when the list of closed schools is being read. There are children desperate to hear that they've got the day off. There are parents, dare I suggest, hoping the head teacher has been out with his shovel and cleared all the snow away. If there's ever any sign of a snow shower anywhere near Norfolk, people are always lightning quick to call in and tell us.

But snow can also be hard work. One evening a heavy snowstorm just before rush hour caused chaos in the centre of Norwich. We went on air at 5pm, planning a normal everyday edition of the *Drive Live* show, but it was soon clear that this was no ordinary evening. The switchboard went crazy, and it turned out the county was so gridlocked and people had so many problems that our two-hour show actually went right through until 10pm.

It was a fine example of people, both inside and outside the office, pulling together to help keep everyone informed. For the entire five hours, the calls never stopped coming – from people with stories of where they were and how long they'd been there to those telling everyone else the spots to avoid. Usually at that time of the day there would not have been many staff in the office, but that evening countless people stayed on duty to go out and report on the problems being caused, and to take the calls coming in, enabling us to keep our information as up to date as possible.

We had all manner of calls that evening: some people had been stranded in cars for hours with children in the back, others had been waiting for ages for buses that never came and there were warnings that ambulances were simply unable to get through the traffic. But it's the more off-the-wall calls that stay with you on nights like that. One woman called to inform us that she'd been caught short to such an extent that she simply had to relieve herself in a stranger's front garden. She was only outdone by the builder who rang to inform us he'd used his hard hat for similar purposes. The trouble was, the small holes in the top of his hat left him with a little more than snow and cold weather to worry about.

I may only have been part of BBC Radio Norfolk for a very short part of its existence, but already I've seen how quickly the industry can change. My first jobs at Norfolk Tower included sitting over a tape machine with a razor blade, literally cutting pieces of tape until they were in a condition that could be used on the air. I wonder whether nowadays you're actually allowed to leave a 16-year-old in sole charge of a razor blade? Well, I won't tell anyone, if you don't. Now, though, everything that we do is done on a computer screen and we've even moved to a different building.

Becoming part of that team today means getting a feeling for the way the station works; what the audience likes and doesn't like. A couple of words often used to describe Radio Norfolk are 'friendly' and 'company'. Many people genuinely see the station, and as a result the people who work there, as friends they welcome into their home for a chat. That can be quite a difficult concept to grasp when you're a nervous teenager contemplating your first steps in broadcasting.

I think you have to have a sense of what has gone before at a radio station like this, if you are to fit in with the general mood and sound of the place. When you're trying to bring your own personal ideas and stamp of individuality to the airwaves, it's important to maintain a respect and appreciation for what has been successful in the past. Knowing a little about the history can only help you come up with the kind of ideas that will keep the audience informed and entertained.

People of all walks of life, especially in these days of fast-moving technological advances, have to be ready to move with the times. Norfolk's local radio station, in that respect, reflects the county as a whole. For example, the Norfolk coast has its unique charms, so that you may well have distinct childhood memories of time spent there. Somewhere like Cromer still maintains the traditional image of crabs and end-of-the-pier shows, but also has to strike that difficult balance of having as modern an attitude as possible, to continue attracting the tourists who keep the local economy booming.

It is a similar thing with radio. We have to make sure the station sounds fresh and different in order to attract new listeners. Yet there's that friendly charm and familiarity, which people hold so dear, that must always be kept at the front of our minds.

It's a particularly volatile time for broadcasting. More and more people are receiving digital radio in their homes, whether through a brand new set, their television or, increasingly, the internet. That all inevitably means much more competition in the battle for listeners, and this is bound to get even more intense as more and more stations become so readily available.

One of the most interesting new gadgets of the twenty-first century has been the Apple iPod. It is really only a high-memory pocket-sized hard disk, engineered to download music through a computer from the internet, but Apple has sold millions, mostly to young people who enjoy being able to carry round with them thousands of music tracks, rather than the 20 or so available on the average CD.

And the iPod has evolved far beyond music. It has given birth to a new form of broadcasting, known as podcasting, which is all the rage in the United States and is catching on here. Podcasting enables organisations or individuals to load sound tracks – speech, music or both – onto the internet, so that they can be downloaded in seconds onto desktop or laptop computers, and onto personal digital assistants, like the BlackBerry, iPod or a mobile phone.

The BBC is already conducting open trials in podcasting, in the belief that its remit is to allow people to access its content by whatever means. Listeners will be able to have new programmes automatically delivered to their computer as soon as they are posted on the web. They just need to download an application such as iPodder that checks the web to find the new version of tagged audio files the listener has already selected.

Speaking at Music Radio 2005, controller of BBC Radio and Music Interactive Simon Nelson said:

These technologies can transform the value we deliver to audiences and make our programmes more accessible for both new and existing audiences. The BBC was the first British broadcaster to podcast, when we made *In Our Time* available in 2004, and our trial in 2005 will enable us to further explore the editorial, technical and distribution issues involved.

It is hoped the project will offer a more detailed picture of audiences' appetite for downloads and information about the kinds of programmes people want to listen to in this way.

The BBC will also include a series of radio programmes in its next trial of the Interactive Media Player (iMP), offering rights protected, time-limited downloads of both television and radio programmes. The iMP aims to give UK residents a television and radio catch-up service for programmes that have been broadcast, as part of the BBC's drive to use new technology to offer even greater public value to licence fee payers.

The BBC World Service already allows anyone with a computer to download its archive of documentaries – an amazing educational resource – as well as its news and public affairs programmes. It is now possible for those ex-pats around the world to listen to Radio Norfolk via the web at bbc.co.uk/norfolk – it's only a matter of time when that will be extended to include programmes 'on demand'.

The mobile phone is also developing fast. It is already possible to download internet radio to mobile phones in wireless hot spots that can be found at fast food outlets, coffee shops, cafés and public places like Norwich and Liverpool Street station. When the railways get round to introducing the next generation of trains, it will be possible to pick up internet radio on rail journeys, including the underground.

Whatever happens, I think there'll always be a demand from people to know what's going on near where they live. They'll want to know why they were stuck in traffic for so long last night, or what the weather's going to be doing tomorrow, so that they can decide whether or not to cut the grass. The amount of competition involved means all stations will be under pressure to come up with new and interesting ways of doing things on the air. I hope that can be achieved without losing the atmosphere, both on the air and behind the scenes, that has evolved at Radio Norfolk over the past 25 years.

Anyone who's ever heard me trying to predict the outcome of football matches on the air will know that my crystal ball has never been in particularly good working order, so I won't even attempt to guess what the next 25 years holds for BBC Radio Norfolk. But if we do all meet back here in 2030, I wonder whether Norwich City will have achieved anything worth another open-top bus tour? Will Nick Bowler have made it into the England cricket team for his fielding ability alone? Will people actually be broadcasting regular football reports from lay-bys on the Acle Straight?

I might not be able to answer those questions, but I am pretty confident in saying we'll all still be fascinated by the weather. If global warming hasn't completely taken over, then I'm sure we'll still live in a place that struggles to deal with snow, and we'll all help each other cope with the journey home and the school closures. Whatever the technology allows us to do 25 years from now, it'll still be the unexpected calls from builders who've come up with novel uses for their hard hats that will linger in the memory.

And Finally

Stephen Bumfrey

2005 is a double celebration year for me. Of course, the balloons and bunting are out for BBC Radio Norfolk, but it was in the autumn of 1980 that I stammered my first-ever words on the wireless. Radio Europa was a pirate station aimed at the tourists on the Italian coast just next door to Monaco. It closed shortly after my arrival and I never did get paid!

By April 1981, I had joined BBC East as a *Look East* studio floor manager and graphic designer. They were kind enough to keep me on and nurture me. I was soon getting involved with BBC Radio Norfolk, making trails and promotions, and eventually getting my first show on Easter Monday 1986. I was as nervous as a chicken doing up his shoelaces in a Paxo factory!

Being an adventurous twenty-something guy, it was only a matter of time before I felt the urge to explore beyond our little corner of the planet: BBC Essex, commercial radio in Birmingham, London and Southampton, an assortment of overseas postings with British Forces Radio BFBS and countless trips to exotic locations, such as India, Australia and Thailand.

I'm not sure why I should have felt so surprised, but I found myself being something of an ambassador for Norfolk. I remember sitting beneath a parasol, with a few beers and a couple of Larnaca Cypriots, explaining how lush and green my gorgeous county is in comparison to the parched beige that surrounded us there in the blazing midday sun. At a dinner party in Hong Kong, I once told a Cantonese gentleman how friendly the folk of a little city called Norwich are. And if you want fresh air, I advised a New Delhi bus driver, you should stand on Gorleston cliffs! Not that I journeyed around the globe insisting on full English breakfasts, a decent cup of tea and none of this foreign rubbish, you understand!

But the truth is, no matter where I was, or how far I travelled, Norfolk was still my place on earth. Then, one day after I'd struggled through the grime, rudeness and tedium that is the London Underground, and hauled myself through the door of my Ealing flat, I decided enough was enough. It was time to go home.

Fifteen years later I was back, and delighted to see that Norwich had moved on, King's Lynn and Great Yarmouth had been given facelifts but, most importantly of all, so much of Norfolk's cultural and natural rural beauty had remained untouched. Yes, we must evolve and keep up with the rest of the world. That is essential. But protecting and savouring our individuality and the land with which we have been blessed must remain at the top of the agenda.

It is inevitable that progress and conservation will regularly lock horns. However, when that happens it is worth remembering that 'once it's gone it's gone'! The days of Norfolk's isolation are a thing of the past, but let us not bow to the quick corporate fix, or the beast of globalisation. Although our dialect will doubtless fade, and our various accents will alter with time, *thar buth wuth haning on tew as lorng as we can. Thass like bein' bi-lingal, intit!* Anywhere else in the EU and we'd receive special funding!

Those born and bred here, and those who have chosen to make Norfolk their home, are rightly proud to be part of a unique and precious expanse of England's green and pleasant land. And all of this reflected daily by BBC Radio Norfolk, a local radio success story. But only because you choose to switch on, write, phone, text and email – and you really do keep us on our toes! Here's to the next 25 years. We thank you!